H

INDIAN COOKING IN A JIFFY

PRASENJEET KUMAR

What People Say........

I have had some really encouraging feedback from my Facebook fans and e-mail subscribers when I shared some of the recipes of this book on my website www.cookinginajiffy.com. Here are some of those comments:

"It is so nice to provide the "Sequencing and Parallel Processing" tips!! It is a very useful tip for the reader to follow!! Keep up the good work and I look forward to learn more from your website!! Thank you very much!!"

Naomi Leung

"I tried out the baked chicken alongwith the garlic bread and soup!!!! my family really enjoyed it!!! thank you so much...!!!"

Gitaa Sharrma

"Thanks so much! I am enjoying your recipes...they are quick to make (in a jiffy!) and easy too. The best thing is that they turn out so tasty! Keep it up! My compliments to you and your mom."

Neena Singh

"The craft always lies in the simplicity of things-- your recipes are like that..."

Surupa Chatterjee

Acknowledgements

This Book is, first of all, dedicated to all those visitors, fans and followers to my website *www.cookinginajiffy.com* as well as to my Facebook and Twitter pages. I'm truly grateful for their really encouraging comments and constructive suggestions that have not only kept my morale high in some really frustrating times but have also resulted into the writing of this book.

It has actually been quite a roller coaster ride since I launched my website in April 2013. Since then, I have been able to bring out my first eBook "How To Cook In A Jiffy: Even If You Have Never Boiled An Egg Before" in September 2013. Its paperback edition was launched in October 2013. Touted as the "easiest cookbook on earth", that book was meant for the complete newbie, who may actually have never boiled an egg before.

It is time to go beyond and address the needs of those who want to now sample "Home Style" Indian cooking. Hence this second book in, what I hope would be, an everlasting "How To Cook Everything In a Jiffy" series of cookbooks.

As usual, I have to dedicate this book to my dearest mom who is the original creator of all these recipes. It is simply amazing how she despite being a working mother (she is actually a very senior Indian Administrative Service officer), finds time to not only cook but also experiment with food.

Most fathers generally leave their wives to cook while they themselves watch television or go out to play golf. However, I have often seen my father helping my mother in the kitchen without any hesitation. The overall objective used to be to cook meals from scratch within 30 minutes, and it was amazing how often we succeeded in meeting this target. As always, the bonus was that cooking time came to be always celebrated, as family time, with lots of cutting, washing, steaming and frying going on side by side with such planning, co-ordination, and sequencing of operations that would put a Mission to Mars to shame! I, therefore, dedicate this book to my father too, who even now takes time off to "advise" me on what my book should focus on, and sometimes even gives editing suggestions.

I finally dedicate this book to all my friends, relatives and acquaintances who have sampled my mom's cooking either at my home or at my work place from my lunch-box and have pestered me to share those recipes. I am especially grateful for their contribution to refining my thoughts on how many kinds of "Home Style" cooking there can be in a complex country like India.

TABLE OF CONTENTS

Chapter 10 Our Sweethearts 221

I

LOOKING FOR INDIAN CUISINE IN LONDON

L et me admit it. Indian cuisine was absolutely the last item on my list when I landed in London, in September 2005, to study Law in University College London (UCL). My first priority was SURVIVAL--- to find food, of any kind, that could soothe somewhat my hunger pangs. So for months if it had to be "plasicky" sandwiches, soulless soups, indifferent salads and endless cups of coffee that I had to subsist on, my attitude was "so be it".

Then the rising expenses and reducing nutrition levels forced me to invest in some really basic pots and pans. Only then could I very hesitatingly take the first, baby steps into "the wonderlands of cooking".

I had to begin at the very beginning, from how to boil (and peel) an egg, to make an egg sandwich, to sauté vegetables, and finally to make a very filling but basic

3-course meal of chicken soup, breaded chicken and garlic toast. If you too are at that level of a complete newbie, you may like to consider starting from my first book "How To Cook In A Jiffy: Even If You Have Never Boiled An Egg Before."

Then I bumped in to Krishna. A year senior to me in St. Stephen's College, Delhi, Krishna too was studying Law, but at the London School of Economics (LSE). He would often be accompanied by Harpal, a Sikh student from Chandigarh, who was studying Economics at LSE. Both were staunch vegetarians which meant they couldn't, unlike me, survive just on soups and sandwiches. I had to appreciate their predicament because I too couldn't think of a college restaurant that could serve at least two different varieties of pure vegetarian sandwiches or soups. Not even the pizzas and ice-creams, I was educated, could be considered vegetarian as they contained cheese and gelatin that had animal origins.

To add salt to injury, both Krishna and Harpal had never tasted such bland food in their lives. Back home, in India, they used to sometimes order "western food" that is, pasta, pizzas or sandwiches but these had never tasted as tasteless as they tasted in the UK. Everything had less salt or perhaps no salt! The vegetables were served boiled, with no spices whatsoever. The desserts too were barely sweet.

Krishna's Hall of Residence did serve, what they called "Indian food" once a week. But these were the typical British interpretations of popular Indian dishes like *Chicken Korma, Chicken Tikka Masala* or *Beef Rogan Josh*. Even if you were not a vegetarian, you could have difficulty finding anything "Indian" about these preparations. For strict vegetarians, of course, there was hardly anything except an occasional "vegetable curry". This was made by sprinkling some kind of an "Indian curry powder" on boiled veggies, just as you sprinkle Parmesan cheese on pasta. This was certainly nothing great to write home about.

The undeniable fact was that, despite putting on a brave front, we were all missing our "Home style" Indian food terribly. Eventually we gathered some courage to venture out looking for 'Indian" restaurants. These, as we soon discovered, were run mostly by immigrants not necessarily from India, but from Bangladesh, Nepal, Sri Lanka, Pakistan, in fact anywhere from the Indian subcontinent. Some of these ramshackle joints, however, did promise that their food will "remind Indians of their home in India".

One day, in Central London, we entered one such restaurant for lunch. The place was run by a very surly Indian (or perhaps he was a Pakistani), who asked us quite coldly what he could do for us. When we asked to look at the Menu card, we were very reluctantly handed over a much used laminated sheet of paper. One quick glance and we knew why the owner was so unenthusiastic about welcoming us Indians. Every dish cost between 20-25 pounds. Even the drinks were more than 5 pounds each. Back home, in India, even 5-star hotels won't dare ask for such prices and this joint was as far from a 5-star property as a London Black Cab would be from a Mercedes.

"Why are Indian dishes so expensive here?" Harpal finally gathered some courage to ask in Hindi.

"Look Man, I don't think the dishes are expensive from British standards. Please also remember that I've to import the masalas and other ingredients from India and that does push up the prices of Indian dishes in the UK", the guy replied, quite in a take-it-or- leave- it attitude.

We exchanged some furtive glances and decided to go ahead with an order for a plate of Mutton Tikka (barbequed lamb) for me, and *Paneer-Mattar* (cottage cheese and peas curry) and rice for Krishna and Harpal. The total bill came to about 50 pounds! When the dishes arrived at our table in about half an hour, I was horrified to see that the Mutton Tikka was almost pink in colour. The meat pieces were also improperly roasted; some looked raw and some looked burnt. To camouflage the dish and to make it supposedly look more attractive to the eye, the cook had put some artificial pink colour!

The *Paneer-Mattar* looked slightly better except that it was very oily. The food was different from what we were getting in our Halls of Residence but was barely satisfactory. The *Paneer-Mattar* also did not taste very fresh to Krishna.

"When was this *Paneer-Mattar* prepared?" inquired Krishna.

"Three days ago" replied the guy, without batting an eyelid.

Shocked, and poorer by 50 Pounds, we vowed never to venture out looking for Indian food in the UK ever again.

Months passed by and we were all becoming more and more home sick and miserable. Krishna specially was terribly missing his "Home Style" Indian food, the smell of the freshly prepared *Sambhar* (split pigeon pea lentils cooked in a south Indian style) served with hot fluffy rice and a vegetable dish.

One day, Harpal's cousin Prakash, who was a manager in a hotel in Inverness, Scotland, met us in London and took us out to Wagamama. Over some really great fusion cuisine, Prakash heard of our misadventures and admitted that he too had similar experiences. The sensible way out, he told us, was to buy ready-made packaged products from Indian stores located in Central London.

Reinvigorated with this tip, we would now regularly buy packaged products like *Paneer-Mattar*, Butter chicken and even *Parathas* (fried Indian unleavened breads). Even though these satiated somewhat our need for Indian food, they could never even come close to fulfilling our desire to have our own Indian "Home Style" food.

II

FINDING "HOME STYLE" FOOD IN INDIA

Came November 2009 and armed with my LLB (Honours) degree and LPC diploma, I was back in India. I had found work as a corporate lawyer with one of the top most Indian law firms. Its swanky office in Central Delhi was close to all the popular restaurants, eating joints as well as the fast food chains of the world.

So food was never a problem. You could have a Pizza from Domino's one day and *Saag*-meat (lamb cooked in pureed spinach) with *Naan* from *Kake Di Hatti* the next. The Chinese joints too were just a stone throw away. Some restaurants even offered a rather sumptuous buffet spread for lunch. This was quite a lifesaver on days when you had missed your breakfast and were really hungry.

Then my parents got posted to Delhi and once again I had access to good and wholesome "Home Food". My office had a dining area equipped with not only some tables and chairs but also a fridge and microwave. So I could now carry a lunch box from home, put it in the fridge the moment I reached office and heat it up in the microwave for lunch during the lunch break.

I noticed that many of my colleagues, who were still living by themselves in rented accommodation, were not following my "example". A senior colleague was continuing to order food either from the office cafeteria or from the Indian fast food joints nearby. The quality of the food used to vary vastly. Some days the food was fresh and the other days not so. Some of us thought that he was just trying to show off, that while he could afford to order food from outside, we lesser mortals couldn't.

That was, of course, very insensitive of us. Once when we were going out for a very important meeting, my senior colleague complained of terrible stomach cramps and bloating. He thought that this was probably because the food, which he had ordered from one of his "preferred" joints the previous day, didn't agree with him. I was sympathetic but some of my junior team members thought he was fibbing to avoid working late that day.

A visit to the doctor, and a few tests that followed, established that my friend was not lying. The culprit, we learnt, was the over fried cooking oil that his favourite food joint was using. We were educated that if any cooking oil is re-heated several times, for example, for frying dishes like *Pooris* (Indian puffed up bread), or *pakodas* (Indian chickpea flour fritters), it breaks down into many harmful fatty acids that can affect sensitive digestive systems adversely.

"Then why don't you carry food from home?" I asked quite concerned.

My friend explained that this was because he did not know any cooking.

"But don't you have a domestic help?" I persisted.

"Oh yes, I do have a part-time maid but she being from the South can't cook the food that I want. May be, when I go to my hometown in Jharkhand next, I will get a help from there who can make my "Home Style" food". My friend explained patiently.

Another colleague was similarly living all by herself in Maharani Bagh, a very posh locality of Delhi. She hated the "greasy Indian fast food", as she described it, that my senior was surviving on. Her solution then was to bring from home some *Dahi* (yoghurt) and chopped papayas for lunch. Again, there were sneers all around. Some alleged that she was getting such "frugal" lunch, because she was perpetually dieting to preserve her statuesque figure.

Lunch time was still fun, with a lot of friendly banters and leg pulling going all-around. Indians also have a very natural tradition of sharing food. So it was not unusual for us to taste a morsel or two from other lunch boxes while we exchanged notes on how nasty a boss or client had been that day.

As mine appeared to be the only "properly assembled" lunch box, I would always get some envious comments from my colleagues about how delicious my lunch box looked and tasted.

"The *Dal* looks so amazing", commented one.

"The smell of fresh basmati rice is so appetising", quipped another.

"Someday I must learn cooking from your mom", declared the third one.

I used to find these comments rather intriguing. I thought I was actually carrying a very simple lunch consisting of some rice, a dal (*Arhar* or split pigeon pea lentils being my favourite) and a vegetable dish (beans steamed with coconut, for example). That too in small quantities just enough for one person. I never thought my lunch box was that great. After all, I had never carried "gourmet dishes" like *Dal Makhni* (lentils with butter), Butter Chicken, or *Kadai Paneer* (Cottage Cheese cooked in a wok) for people to say wow!

It suddenly dawned on me that the "eating-out" culture that was becoming so pervasive was making basic Home-style Indian cooking into some kind of a rarity. In olden days, women usually learnt cooking from their mothers and continued cooking at their in-laws. Domestic help trained and supervised by such mothers and daughters-in-law too knew how to cook "Home Style" food to the liking of everyone in the house. In those days, restaurant curries were considered a delicacy.

The ever changing fast paced modern lifestyle is making basic Home style Indian cuisine either extinct or a very unattainable distant dream for both Indian students abroad and employees working in India. People living by themselves either don't know how to cook or don't have enough time to cook at home. Higher wages in the corporate sector means that almost everyone can afford to order food from outside.

There is naturally a price to pay for this "convenience" ranging from obesity and gastrointestinal disorders to diabetes and high blood pressure. There is also a limit to how many times you can have "gourmet restaurant style curries" in a day no matter how much you may seem to think you like them.

A greater concern appeared to stem from the perception that Indian cuisine is complicated and time consuming. Unfortunately, quite a few cookbooks had a hand in spreading this misconception. They do that by suggesting either too many exotic ingredients or to cook certain dishes for hours together which makes Indian food less doable for busy couples.

No doubt, Indian cuisine is very diverse in nature. Even the *dals* (lentils) that Indians have almost every day is so different. For example, the dal I used to carry was the simplest, tempered just with *ghee* (clarified butter) and *jeera* (cumin seeds). My colleagues from Mumbai were, however, tempering theirs with black mustard seeds and curry leaves. The South-Indian twist on the same dal meant the really spiced up *Sambhar* that not only contained black mustard seeds and curry leaves but also, what to me looked like, a hundred other fiery and very colourful ingredients.

And yet, there was a unifying thread in this maddening diversity, in the sense that we all were having some kind of a dal in our different versions of "Home Food".

III

HOW IS "HOME STYLE" INDIAN FOOD DIFFERENT FROM "RESTAURANT FOOD"?

Many of my international friends are surprised to learn that there is in India a distinct difference between "Home Style" food and "restaurant food".

"So, what do you Indians eat at home?" They will ask me.

Is it all really so different from "restaurant food"?

And, more importantly, is it so superior to "restaurant food" that it deserves to be discussed as a separate category?

I believe that such a "strange" debate among Europeans or Englishmen does not take place in the western world (though I may be wrong!). There you usually look up to the versions created in restaurants and by Michelin Star chefs of say "Roast Turkey" and try to replicate it at home. Here, in India, you almost look down upon the versions of say, "yellow dal" peddled by restaurants and very condescendingly declared your own "Home Style" versions to be less oily or more tasteful and decidedly superior in any case.

I also discovered that certain dishes are just not available in restaurants. For example, I couldn't have my Eastern Indian style *Arhar dal* anywhere in India including the wayside eateries in Bihar and Uttar Pradesh. Similarly, the *Dahi-Sarson* (yogurt-mustard) fish, which every Bengali household can probably offer, is unavailable even in 5-star hotels in Delhi. Why, even the simple Indian unleavened bread called *Chapati* or *Phulka*, that I eat every day, would be absent from most restaurant menus who prefer to offer *Tandoori Roti* or *Naan* instead.

Digging a little deeper, I learnt that the whole style of restaurant cooking in India is diametrically opposed to what we practice in our homes with respect to the same dish. For restaurants, speed is of utmost essence as they don't expect any customer to wait for longer than 15 minutes to be served. So they have to keep ingredients ready in a semi-finished condition for a quick conversion in to whatever dish the customer demands. Chicken, for example, will be semi-cooked in a *tandoor* and then kept ready to be converted into Butter Chicken or Chicken Tikka or *Chicken Do Pyaza* (Chicken with two onions literally!) at the drop of a hat. Same goes for the veggies, which will be cut, and even boiled, to be used for any curried or dry version of that vegetable dish. This is the only way for restaurants to come up with menus that contained sometimes as many as 100 dishes.

A *dhaba* (roadside eatery) doesn't even have that luxury of a lead time of 15 minutes. Their customers being mostly busy (and burly) truck drivers from Punjab don't like to wait even for 5 minutes before being served. So a good *dhaba* to survive has to cook and keep ready its full repertoire of 10-12 dishes all the while. That way it is quite like the "Home Food" which too is fully finished in one go, starting from scratch. The one big difference, however, is that *dhaba* food would contain a lot more oil than home cooked meals. This is so because oil acts as some kind of preservative for *dhaba* food which, unlike home cooked meals, doesn't normally go into a fridge.

It was for this reason, it dawned on me, that even the Indian desserts like *Gulab Jamuns* or *Jalebis* served in *dhabas* would be fried!

The upshot of all this very fascinating debate that we carried over many, many moons was the conclusion that there is still a very robust tradition of "Home Style" cuisine alive and kicking in India. And this was very different from Indian restaurant cooking because:

One, it was cooked from scratch, from fresh ingredients;

Two, many "Home Style" dishes were simply NOT available on restaurant menus;

Three, it was much healthier as it allowed full freedom to change your salt, sugar and spice levels;

Four, it was not only less oily but it also permitted you to choose your preferred oil (mustard, olive, coconut, ground nut, soya, sunflower, rice bran or whatever...); and above all,

Five, it was less complicated and, therefore, easier to cook.

For me, and for all my colleagues in India, who just couldn't turn into professional chefs overnight, the last point was an eye opener.

"Is that so?" many asked incredulously.

"Prove it, Prasenjeet"; someone threw a challenge.

So I picked up the gauntlet and ventured out to start with a catalogue of my own family's "Home Style" Indian cuisine.

And this Book is the result of that small, modest attempt to do that.

You will find lots of quick and easy Home-style Indian recipes in this book (along with sequencing and parallel processing described fully later on) that will help you put together a four course Indian meal (consisting of a rice, dal, two vegetable dishes or one vegetarian and one non-vegetarian dish) in less than 30 minutes (literally in a jiffy!)

Please remember that the "Home Style" recipes that I have catalogued here are made regularly in my home. You are strongly encouraged to experiment, adapt and add your own variation so that the food tastes like your "Home food".

A word of warning though. If you are a complete newbie i.e. someone who does not even know how to boil an egg, then I suggest you start from my first book "How To Cook In A Jiffy Even If You Have Never Boiled An Egg Before" (see the excerpt towards the end of this book). Indian cooking can be a little tricky and it is best to acquire some basic cooking skills before making this a part of your daily routine.

CHAPTER 1

HOW TO SET UP YOUR VERY BASIC KITCHEN

L et me assure at the very beginning that you can rustle up an Indian meal in whatever kind of kitchen you may already have.

But in case, you have to set up a kitchen afresh, we are listing below some equipment that a reasonably functional kitchen should have.

The list is purely suggestive. Please feel free to add or delete as per your actual requirement.

Absolute Essentials

Stove/Heat Source: The first thing you would need in your kitchen would be a stove/heat source which could run on electricity or gas. If your kitchen is "bare" (as in many countries like India), you naturally have to first invest into this device. At the simplest level, you may have to choose among a four burner, two burner or even a single burner model. The price difference between the various models may not be much but in my experience, it is always advisable to pick up at least a two burner version if you intend to cook a full meal. Otherwise for making simple one dish items, even a single burner stove should suffice.

Kadhai (Wok): This contraption is excellent for making a wide variety of Indian dishes as the wide open mouth makes it very easy to stir or deep fry anything, with less oil too. You can have a non-stick one or even an anodised one. It is suggested that you have at least two woks of different sizes.

Deep Non-Stick Pan: You need this for sautéing vegetables, boiling/ poaching chicken and fish or even for boiling water.

Shallow Non-Stick Pan: This is suggested as it is easier to make omelettes, scrambled egg, fried eggs in a shallow pan.

Grater: This is required for grating cheese and some vegetables which might require grating.

Wooden Spatulas: At least two for stirring and taking out the cooked stuff from your non-stick pan. Remember if you use a stainless steel spatula, you will scratch the non-stick/Teflon coating of the pan in no time and spoil it.

Stainless Steel Slotted Spoon: This helps in not only stirring the food well but also in draining excess oil when taking out fried things like *pooris* (Indian puffed up bread) or *pakodas* (Indian chickpea flour fritters) from the wok.

Sharp Knives: At least two, preferably in two different coloured handles, one for cutting vegetables, including onions and garlic, and a separate one for cutting fruits. I am suggesting this because onions and garlic leave such a pungent smell that even after the knife has been washed, the smell can get transferred to the fruit or nuts you may be cutting for your dessert. Unless you love having your cut apples with a garlic smell (ha, ha)!!

Cutting Board: For cutting vegetables, fruits and anything else that might need chopping. Again, if you could have a separate one for your meats, it would be more hygienic.

A Rolling Pin (Belan) and a Rolling Board (Chakla): Only if you intend making any Indian breads like *roti*, *poori* or *paratha*, this would be an essential item. However, if you only want to stick to rice dishes then you need not bother.

A Few Bowls: For beating eggs, keeping cut vegetables, etc.

Crockery and Cutlery: Enough for serving and eating food for as many persons as you desire.

Optional As Your Needs Expand

Blender/Grinder: You may like to invest in this category to help you have dishes like smoothies, milk shakes, cold coffee, soups and also to make pastes of items like onion, garlic, ginger essential for making Indian curries.

Microwave/Oven: Indian dishes are not very amenable to being cooked in either a microwave or oven. But nothing can beat a microwave in re-heating food. Also many dishes requiring a tandoor (an earthen oven) can be easily replicated in an oven. So, if you can afford one, a combo microwave-cum-oven can be a useful addition to your kitchen.

Refrigerator: This is absolutely essential for storing both cooked and fresh food. The freezer not only makes ice and preserves your ice cream but is essential for storing excess food which you may like to eat after a few days or even weeks. It also can store frozen raw chicken, fish and meat saving you from making many unnecessary trips to the supermarket.

Dish Washer: This takes away the drudgery of cleaning up your dishes after you are done with cooking and eating.

Rice Maker: This appliance not only helps making rice idiot-proof but also keeps it hot and fluffy till you are ready to eat it.

Pressure Cooker: In India, especially if you wish to cook in a JIFFY, this device would be considered an absolute essential. If you are alone, a three litre (approx. 6 US pint liquid) size is alright. But if you are a family of three or four, then a five litre (approx. 11 US pint liquid) size is suggested.

As use of pressure cookers arouses strong emotions both in its favour and against, I'm putting pressure cookers in the optional list.

But let's discuss this topic a little more for the benefit of those who are not very familiar with a pressure cooker's operations.

CHAPTER 2

TO USE OR NOT TO USE A PRESSURE COOKER

Many readers have written asking why I recommend the use of pressure cookers in many of my Indian recipes when pressure cookers have quite the "bad boy" reputation of being inherently dangerous. Also whether using pressure cookers is "mandatory" if you wish to "cook in a JIFFY."

To the first part of the question, my general answer would be that yes, using sub-standard pressure cookers can be dangerous but only as dangerous as sub-standard microwaves, electric kettles or gas stoves can be. In fact, an ill-maintained kitchen can be a very dangerous place for anyone, especially small children.

But to the second part, I have to admit that Indians, from slum dwellers to millionaires, love using pressure cookers simply because nothing can cook food faster. Pressure cookers are fast because they cook at the temperature of steam—at over 120 degree Centigrade (or 248 Degree Fahrenheit), and not at the temperature of water that boils around 100 degree Centigrade (or 212 degree Fahrenheit) that open non-pressurised vessels like woks and pans work with.

Just on that count, Pressure cookers can be termed "green" because they help save fuel, which in any case is becoming more and more expensive, especially in countries like India. In addition, pressure cookers are considered to preserve nutrition better which is otherwise lost when food is cooked over extended periods of time. Because of these higher temperatures, pressure cookers are also believed to kill bacteria and breakdown many a pesticide or chemical that our food may often be contaminated with.

On the negative side, using pressure cookers certainly requires a little more manual effort than pushing buttons on a microwave or an oven. You also need some dexterity and practice to make sure that the lid fits well, otherwise the cooker may not attain full pressure. Finally, when using a microwave or oven, you can select a programme and leave the kitchen, if you so wish for the selected time, to watch TV or whatever. But you should NEVER ever leave a pressure cooker unattended as it will not switch off on its own like a microwave or an oven does! This may not be a problem if you are attending to some other tasks in the kitchen in a "parallel processing" mode, to really help cook in a JIFFY.

For occasional cooking of Indian dishes, I won't recommend that any one should invest in a pressure cooker. Even in India, most of the road side eateries (*dhabas*) practice all kinds of alternate ways to cook without using pressure cookers. These include marinating the meats or pre-soaking the *dals* (lentils). The Chinese practice of cutting meats in thin slices, or mincing it, is also a sure shot way to ensure that your meats cook well, in woks or pans, without a pressure cooker.

If you do decide to use a pressure cooker, a tip from my experience is to eat "pressure cooked food" after a while, say after 1-2 hours, if you can help it, as I find this enhances flavours. This may be because the time gap allows all flavours to seep in properly.

As for recommending a good brand of a pressure cooker, I'd rather not suggest any, as brands and their reputation vary from country to country. Just pick up a pressure cooker that meets all your local safety standards and is manufactured and serviced by a reputed company.

But then this prescription should apply to every gadget that we use in our households every day, shouldn't it?

CHAPTER 3

AN INTRODUCTION TO SOME BASIC INDIAN SPICES

It is easy to be overwhelmed with the sheer number and variety of fresh herbs and spices that are commonly used in Indian cuisine. I shouldn't, therefore, make this topic even more complicated by giving the scientific or botanical names of such spices, or where they grow, or how these are harvested and processed. There are many excellent books who have done better justice to this topic.

What I shall attempt here is to just list out some twenty of these spices that you should experiment with when you are just starting out with "Home Style" Indian cooking. The ones in *bold* are essential for any authentic Indian kitchen. The rest are optional.

The discerning reader may notice the omission of *Kastoori Methi* (a very fragrant variety of Fenugreek) which is very popular for making curries in Indian restaurants. That's precisely the reason why I am leaving this out from my list. But if you prefer your food to taste like *dhaba* food, do go ahead and stock on *Kastoori Methi* too. Just remember that this is such a strong herb that it will drown the fragrance of all other spices, howsoever expensive they may be. So for heavens, don't use your saffron with *Kastoori Methi* ever!

I am also leaving out some expensive spices like nutmeg or star aniseed as they are hardly ever used in your day-to-day cooking.

Here is then my list, in alphabetical order:

Amchur (Dried green mango powder): This is used for imparting a strong sour taste.

Asafoetida (Hing): This is used in small quantities for imparting a strong smell. It is considered very healthy for digestive purposes though some people may find the smell unpleasant and strong. Don't use your saffron with *Hing*, therefore, ever!

Bay Leaves (Tej Patta): Used as a flavouring agent.

Cardamom (Elaichi): These come in two varieties: one is small, pale-green and the other is large and brown/black. The pale green variety is used in many Indian dishes including desserts. The brown variety is used for making curries or *pulaos*, but not in sweetmeats.

Chilli (Kashmiri Red variety): In our recipes, we have suggested the use of Kashmiri Red Chillies as these impart a nice red colour and are not as hot as are the other red chillies. In case, you like your food to be really hot, then you can use the other red chillies available in the market which are much hotter.

Cinnamon (Dalchini): This looks like the thin bark of a tree and imparts a lovely flavour both to the sweet and curried dishes. In India, however, it is more used for curries as Indians like Cardamom in their desserts much more than Cinnamon.

Cloves (Laung): These look like dried flower buds and add a lovely flavour to the food. Cloves are supposed to have antiseptic qualities which helps preserve food.

Coconut (Nariyal) powder or milk: This is used commonly in many South Indian and coastal Indian preparations.

Coriander seeds and fresh green leaves (Dhania and Dhania patta): The dried seeds of Coriander form an essential part of Indian curries and are used quite extensively. The fresh green leaves are used for making Chutneys (Indian sauce) as well as for sprinkling on curries. Since the fresh leaves have a strong flavour, they should only be used by those who really like it.

Cumin seeds (Jeera): Cumin is another essential ingredient of Indian cuisine and is generally the first spice to go into the heated cooking oil before other items are added.

Curry leaves (Kare-patta): These leaves have a lovely flavour and are absolutely essential if you like South Indian cuisine. In India, it grows in abundance and so is easily the cheapest herb to use. Generally used fresh, these can also be dried and used as they retain much of their fragrance even in the dried form.

Fennel (Saunf): This is used for making some dishes and forms a part of the *Pach Phoran* (which shall be discussed later).

Fenugreek (Methi): These are small flat seeds which have a slightly bitter flavour and must be used for only in the quantities prescribed. They add quite a piquant flavour to the curries or dry dishes they are added to which are liked by many Indians. Lately, Fenugreek has acquired quite a cult status because of its almost magical effect in reducing the severity of Diabetes.

Garam Masala: This is a mixture in equal quantities of cinnamon, cloves, cardamom (both pale-green and brown variety) and whole black pepper corns. These can be ground together and kept in air tight containers for future use for up to a week. Some dishes can also be made by putting the whole spices in oil/ clarified butter (*Ghee*).

All lovers of Indian cooking must learn to use this mixture properly. If you cook Indian dishes only occasionally, you may be tempted to use the commercially available *Garam Masala* powders. Please remember, however, that to economise on costs, some manufacturers skimp on the more expensive ingredients mentioned above and instead add lots of coriander powder, cumin powder, turmeric powder, red chilli powder etc. to add volume. They even add *Kastoori Methi* which just drowns the subtle flavours of other *Garam Masalas*. So do check before you buy such a ready mix of spices.

Mustard seeds black (Rai): These are black mustard seeds which look the same as the yellow variety but are supposed to be more pungent than their yellow cousins. This mustard seed is used a lot in South Indian and Western Indian cooking.

Onion seeds dried (Mangrela or Kalonji): This spice is generally used as a part of the *Pach Phoran* (which is discussed below).

Pachphoran: Literally, a mixture of five spices namely black mustard seeds, cumin seeds, fenugreek seeds, fennel seeds and dried onion seeds, mixed in equal proportion, this category is regularly used in quite a few Eastern Indian dishes.

Saffron (Kesar): Easily the most expensive spice in the world, this comes from the stamen of the saffron flower. It has thread like strands in dark orange colour which when dissolved in milk or water gives out its colour along with its mild, earthy flavour. Not a spice to be used casually, saffron is used mostly in making desserts and some exotic dishes.

Turmeric (Haldi): This is easily the commonest and the most important ingredient in any Indian curry dish. Though it does not have much of a flavour, it has a dark yellow colour and a lot of therapeutic value.

Yoghurt (Dahi): Not really a spice or herb, yoghurt is frequently used in many Indian dishes. The variety used in cooking is cultured yoghurt and is always unflavoured. That way it comes closest to the Greek variety of yoghurt.

CHAPTER 4

WHAT OTHER STRANGE THINGS DO YOU NEED TO KNOW ABOUT INDIAN CUISINE?

India is a land of strange sights, sounds, smells, customs, traditions, and of course cuisine. But regardless of where you go in India, you will find some common thread binding its varied culinary traditions together. I underline a few here.

Eating in Thalis: Traditionally, Indian food used to be served in *Thalis* (round platters), that is everything, from starters to desserts would be served in one go. That is how it is still done on weddings, or on such special occasions, in many parts of India. The guests usually sit on the floor, cross legged and are served on a banana leaf or on plates made of broad leaves.

Food, if not served in one go in a *Thali*, would be served on your leaf plate in a continuous stream. At the end of it all, the leaf plates along with the food remnants will be fed to the cows, thus earning merit for all concerned. No dishwashing, and the most environmentally benign waste disposal possible, you will have to salute the ancient Indians for thinking of everything!

If you would like to sample a typical North Indian or South Indian *Thali*, do look out for a branch of restaurant chains like *Sagar Ratna, Naivedyam, Rajdhani* etc. or ask your local hosts for suggestions, when you are next in India.

No Soup, Dal a distant substitute: As you'd immediately notice, soups don't precede a normal Indian meal. In a multi-cuisine restaurant, if you insist, you may be offered a Western or Chinese soup. Some try to even take out the curry from any yoghurt based Chicken dish and serve its diluted version as Chicken *Shorba* (soup). The British came up with a lentil based Mulligatawny soup but it still hasn't become mainstream.

India being a tropical country, it was probably not necessary to serve soup in the beginning of a meal to warm you up. It is surprising, however, that even culinary traditions of the colder areas, for example in the Himalayan region of India, too don't serve any soup. *Kashmiris* and *Garhwalis* have all kinds of curries but no soup. The nearest thing to soup that the *Kashmiris* and *Ladakhis* have is their salted tea, but that they have it all-through-the-day and almost never before a meal!

Indian cuisine also doesn't involve boiling its meats and veggies first and then thinking about what to do with the stock thereof. Stock is part and parcel of the Indian curry. And then you have the formidable variety of dals that Indians cook. So who needs soups?

Carbs are central not meats: If you see an Indian eating at a *dhaba*, you will immediately notice that rice and breads would be forming more than 60% of that meal. The balance 40% would be distributed over meats, veggies and lentils.

Western cuisine will traditionally reverse this proportion in favour of the meats. One reason could be that Europe's prolonged winters, and consequently shorter cultivating season, meant that they could rely less on grains.

Most of the Indian sub-continent, and even the South-East Asian countries had no such constraints. They could easily have two crops, and sometimes even three. Islands like Bali could sow and reap paddy whenever they wanted. But the moment you go to the colder areas of China or Central Asia, you will find meat gaining the upper hand.

Now that the world economies have integrated so much that you can choose what you can put in your meal platter, what should one do? If you have too much meat, you may exceed your protein requirement and invite problems like high cholesterol, renal stones and even Gout. On the other hand, if you have too much of carbs, you could have more calories than your body needs, suffer from protein shortage, become overweight and could be prone to diabetes.

Why not then balance your carbs with proteins and follow, as Lord Buddha advised some 2600 years back, the MIDDLE PATH?

Curries are compulsory: This is so obvious that you just can't miss it. Anywhere you go and you will find curries dominating the Indian meal platter.

Why is it so? One reason could be the need to have lots of water in a tropical country like India. This curries could meet in a very healthy (you are boiling your water after all, aren't you) and appetizing a manner. The second reason could be that if you are growing so much rice you would need some curry to "wet" it, to make it less sticky and more palatable.

This could be the reason that you have curries in all rice growing regions of the world, even in Thailand, Laos or Myanmar. On the other hand, the non-rice growing and wheat-eating colder areas of China, Afghanistan and Central Asia rely more on barbeques and didn't have much need for curries.

Sweets and salty dishes can be eaten together: This happens, I suppose, because in the

Thali style of food service there is no way of stopping what you eat first and then next. Certainly in the perfectly democratic world of the Indian cuisine, when you have access to a bevy of salty, sweet, bitter, sour and hot dishes, you also have the full freedom to decide what you want to eat, with what and when. So you will often see children soothing their taste buds with a spoonful of the sweet dish, whenever they would have had a taste of something bitter or hot. Then you would have the somewhat strange spectacle of *Gujaratis* eating their desserts first and the main meal later.

In temples, you will often be served *Poori-Kheer* (unleavened Indian fried bread with rice pudding) or *Poori-Halwa* (unleavened Indian fried bread with flour dessert) as *prasadam* (blessings).

Can you think of anyone eating an apple pie with roast chicken (together and not as a separate course) anywhere in the world? I'd certainly love to be educated.

Spices not sprinkled on but cooked with: In Indian cuisine, you don't cook something first and then sprinkle some spices on it to make it somewhat palatable. Spices almost always have to be cooked with the main meal to unleash their full flavours and magic.

Sauces not prepared separately: It is again a very common practice in Western cuisine to boil or bake something first and then to pour on it a tomato or cheese based sauce or flambé it with some wine or such other alcoholic beverage.

In India, only restaurants semi cook their meats and vegetables and prepare some sauces separately; both to be mixed the moment someone asks for a tomato or onion or yoghurt based dish. This is because for restaurants, speed is of utmost essence. So they have to keep ingredients ready in a semi-finished condition for a quick conversion in to whatever dishes the customers demand.

However, "Home Style" (or even *dhaba*) Indian food is made in one go with everything cooked together. The only thing to "finish" a curry dish could be the sprinkling of some Coriander (Cilantro) leaves. Similarly, *dals* are tempered later with *Ghee* (clarified butter) and *Jeera* (Cumin seeds) or *Rai* (black mustard seeds).

But these are not exactly sauces that are prepared first and poured on to a cooked dish.

Taste buds continuously titillated with accompaniments like pickles, chutneys, raita, papad......: Foreigners are aghast at the sheer number of titbits that literally litter a typical Indian *Thali*. So you will have pickles, made from vegetables, fruits, and even fish. Then you have all kinds of *Papadums, Baris* or *Tilauris* made from lentils. Added to these would be the home made sauces called *Chutneys* and sweet marmalade like preparations made from some fruits called

Murabbas. And in North India, how can you forget the yoghurt based *Raitas*?

Once a European friend asked me if these accompaniments didn't "confuse" your taste buds unnecessarily.

Well, to be frank, they do. But Indians love that "confusion", because as I've already mentioned, an ideal Indian meal must have a balance of all tastes—sour, salty, bitter, hot and sweet.

And the best way to ensure that is by adding accompaniments which are generally readymade (like jams, marmalades and sauces in the West) and don't have to be cooked at the last moment.

Less use of ovens or barbeques: Except in the Northern Indian states like Punjab, where buried-in-the-earth ovens called *Tandoor* are very popular, there has hardly been any tradition of baking in the mainstream Indian cuisine. Boiling, frying, steaming-- is all there but whatever little barbequing and baking is done, appears to have come to India from Persia, Turkey or the Central Asian regions from where many Muslim rulers of India had come.

Again, I believe, weather played a part here. Europe and many other colder areas of the world had to keep some kind of fire going in their homes all the while to keep them warm. It was a matter of time, therefore, when someone stumbled upon an appliance that could be attached to the fireplace to cook or rather bake things without much supervision. Even the smoke that resulted from such fireplaces was discovered to have the ability to cure, dry and preserve meats and again mainstream Indian cuisine has no tradition of having such "smoked" meats.

But don't worry. Globalization has ensured that whatever cakes, pies, breads or pizzas you crave for, you will find it available on the Indian shop shelves today.

Chopsticks can't work, cutlery is optional: Chopsticks don't work with Western cuisine either because for that meats or vegetables have to be cut into chopstick-friendly sizes first. Cutlery too is hardly used when you eat a Burger or a Pizza, especially while walking to your office. But can you avoid cutlery in formal dinners?

Well, in India, even in many 5-star hotels, you have to specifically ask for cutlery in their signature Indian restaurants. In weddings, your *Thali* may contain just one spoon for the dessert, if you are lucky.

Many of my European friends can't imagine how you can pick up rice with your fingers and take it to your mouth without half of it falling on the way. To that, I invite them to come and see how expert South Indians can pick up a curry too from their plates (and not their bowls) with their fingers. It's a sight you must not miss while in India.

Till then, just ask for whatever cutlery you need for your Indian meal. You will at least get a spoon, I promise.

Vegetarian dishes mimic the non-vegetarian taste: This happens all the while in the West with soya sausages mimicking the taste and flavours of pork or chicken sausage, for example.

In India, this mimicking takes place in two ways. First, where the non-vegetarian portions of a dish would just be dropped. For example, the popular mutton *Shami Kebab* would be made exactly with the same ingredients but without the mutton mince. You can't do the same with chicken sausage, after dropping the chicken mince, can you?

In the second, you have totally vegetarian versions which are sometimes more prolific than their non-vegetarian counterparts. For example, the normal non-vegetarian *koftas* would be made either with mutton or chicken mince. But its vegetarian versions, trying to mimic the same texture, flavour and taste, would be made of bottle gourd (*Lauki ke Kofte*), jackfruit (*Kathal ke Kofte*), reduced milk (*Khoya ke Kofte*) or one of the lentils (*Moong dal ke Kofte*).

Anoothi Vishal, a noted food critic, has a "hypothesis that this intriguing strain of cooking originated especially to cater to (such matriarchs) who must have surely been interested enough in the relatively more exotic and intricate non-vegetarian dishes that were being cooked up at home but did not want to give up on their religious/caste injunctions."

Be that as it may, do try these beguiling dishes that try to taste like meat dishes, when you are next in India.

Cinnamon is not used in desserts but, you guessed it, in curries: Do you know that Cinnamon (or the Indian *Dalchini*) is one spice that is used both in Eastern (including Indian) as well as Western cuisines?

Indian cuisine is well known to use a mind-numbing variety of spices (the list is indeed long). I have heard quite a few celebrity chefs boasting how a particular kebab recipe of theirs uses thirty-six (or thirty-nine, I don't remember) spices as ingredients. That would be quite an overkill, in my opinion, and I'd definitely not recommend that any casual dabbler in Indian cuisine experiments with more than ten spices in one dish. But, as I said, that's just my personal opinion.

Coming back to Cinnamon, however, I can bet that this would definitely be in that long list of spices that our celebrity chefs use to create their exotic Indian dishes. I am not sure whether any of their remaining 35 or 38 spices would be so definitely used in Western cuisine. I have always wondered, therefore, as to why Cinnamon is one of the few exceptions.

There is no doubt that Cinnamon does impart a lovely flavour to any dish. Who can resist the aroma of a freshly baked Apple Pie, Pumpkin pie or a Cinnamon roll!

This brings me to the next interesting difference that in the West Cinnamon is used for preparing sweet things like desserts and pies. In India, however, it is more used for savoury things like curries, as Indians prefer Cardamom or Saffron in their desserts more. Cinnamon in fact occupies a pride of place in the preparation of the Indian *garam masala*, a spice mixture that is commonly used in chicken curry, *pulaos, biryanis*, vegetable dishes, or even *rajma* or kidney beans curry. *Kashmiris* put Cinnamon powder in their tea which they call "*Kehwa*" that is usually served after dinner. Many claim that adding a teaspoon of Cinnamon and honey in your morning tea would protect you from common cold and stomach worries.

That's actually an excellent suggestion from my personal experience.

You can cook with yoghurt: Eating yoghurt is, of course, no big deal. Flavoured or unflavoured, frozen or thawed, plain or fortified with probiotics, made from full cream or skimmed milk----the variety that industrially manufactured yoghurt today comes in is simply mindboggling.

But cooking with yoghurt? You cook with cheese and wine but yoghurt--the question would certainly stump most aficionados of European or American or even Chinese or Thai schools of cooking.

But talk to anyone from any part of India, and you would instantly get a whole list of regional dishes that use yoghurt in quite a "matter-of-fact" way. This is because before tomatoes were brought to India by the Portuguese sometimes in the 16th century, yoghurt was the main ingredient (apart from tamarind and pomegranate seeds) that could add a little sour taste to Indian dishes.

In Kashmir, savour the *wazwan* (a feast usually served on special occasions like weddings) and you'd find the pride of place accorded to *Gushtabbas* (pounded boneless meat balls cooked in yoghurt) or *Yakhni or Dhania Kormas* (both containing mutton pieces, with bones, cooked in yoghurt, with different spices).

In western Indian states of Maharashtra or Gujarat, *Kadhi* (made from yoghurt or butter milk with added potato, onions or vegetable fritters) would be omnipresent in all vegetarian platters. Punjabi vegetarians too like a slightly different version of this *Kadhi* but they actually use copious amounts of yoghurt in their popular drink *Lassi* (basically a yoghurt shake).

The Punjabis (as well as the other North-Indian meat eaters) also like to marinate their chicken and mutton with yoghurt before they put it in their *tandoors* (earthen ovens) or barbeques, or even curries. Yoghurt in these regions is also supposed to bring in good luck as there is a tradition of NOT leaving your house for any long journey or an examination/interview without having at least a spoonful of yoghurt with sugar.

The East, specially the Bengal region, is famous for cooking their fish in yoghurt. Just check out their dishes of *Dahi-Machhli* (fish cooked in yoghurt and *garam masala*) or *Dahi-sarson* (fish cooked in a yoghurt-mustard sauce). Their yoghurt dessert *Mishti-doi* (literally sweet yoghurt) or *Bhapa-doi* (steamed yoghurt) is simply out-of-this-world.

The southern regions of India are so fond of yoghurt that they usually end their meals, not with a dessert, but with curd-rice. Yoghurt is also a very important ingredient of the south-Indian coconut *chutney* that goes well with south-Indian snacks like *Idlis, Vadas and Dosas.*

CHAPTER 5

RICE & INDIAN BREADS

Carbs like rice, wheat, corn and millets have for centuries occupied a more central position in Indian cuisine than meats. No Indian can think of going to bed after gorging on just a piece of steak, howsoever generous it may be. He will also not be satisfied if the steak were accompanied with some French fries. For him, the proper accompaniment for a steak or any other meat or vegetable dish would be rice or *rotis*.

And here too, the carbs will have the majority share, at more than 50% on your plate. Of course, at restaurants, you can let your meats (or veggies) occupy this majority position, but no "Home Style" Indian platter would be considered complete without a generous helping of some kind of rice and a *roti* or two, if possible.

There would, as usual, be mindboggling ways to cook your rice and breads in all kinds of regional flavours and styles. For "Home Style" cooking, however, we suggest a mastery over a smaller list of just ten varieties, namely:

Boiled Rice—for everyday use in all parts of India;

Curd Rice or Lemon Rice —for the South Indians;

Onion Rice, *Jeera* Rice or Peas *Pulao*— for those special occasions;

Khichdi—for the Saturdays, for religious reasons or whenever you want a complete meal in one dish;

Roti, Chapati or Phulka—for everyday use;

Parathas or Pooris—for picnics and celebratory occasions.

Let's then get into the nitty-gritties of how to prepare these ten foundation carb dishes of any "Home Style" platter.

Rice Boiled

Ingredients

Rice-1 glass

Water-2 glasses (if using mature and flavourful basmati rice, otherwise 1.5 glasses)

Tip: Use the same glass please! Otherwise, your rice will NOT turn out to be fluffy.

Method using a pressure cooker

Wash the rice well (*in a vessel 3-4 times, but don't rub it lest the grains break*) and let it naturally "dry", on an inclined plate, for 15-20 minutes. This helps enhance the aroma.

In a pressure cooker (3-5 litre capacity or 6-11 US pints liquid capacity) bring the water to a boil.

Add the rice to the boiling water.

Close the lid of the pressure cooker BUT remove the *weight*.

When steam starts escaping from the vent (*don't worry, you will hear that typical sound*), reduce the heat to minimum. In other words, if cooking on gas, turn the knob to SIM (mer).

Wait for 10 minutes and switch off the gas. Take out the rice. Your hot fluffy rice is ready.

Method using a thick bottomed vessel/deep pan

In a vessel or a pan, bring the water to a boil.

Add the rice to the boiling water. Turn the heat to low and cover the vessel/deep pan with a well-fitting lid.

Cook for 15-20 minutes without stirring the rice. Switch off the heat source. Lift the lid and check whether the rice is properly cooked.

Cooked rice is always soft. To check, you have to take out a grain of rice and press it between your fingers (obviously use a spoon to take out the grain to avoid scalding your hands). If the grain is still hard, that means it is under cooked. If it is soft, then it is cooked properly. In case the grain is not properly cooked, you may like to add another ½ cup of water and let it cook on low heat for another 7-10 minutes.

Traditional method (the way it is cooked in villages or dhabas even today)

In a vessel or a pan, bring three (instead of two mentioned in the above two methods) glasses of water (for one glass of rice) to a boil.

Add the rice to the boiling water. Turn the heat to medium and don't cover the vessel/deep pan, because the water will boil and spill over.

Cook for 15-20 minutes stirring the rice gently from time to time. Keep on checking whether the rice is properly cooked.

Once the rice is done, switch off the heat source. Drain all the excess water. (You can use a colander. Traditionally, the vessel will just be covered with a lid and the water poured out. This is tricky as both the vessel and the water would be very hot.)

Although the traditional method takes more time, it is believed to bring out the flavours better. Since the water used for boiling the rice is totally drained out, some dieticians claim that this method helps take out some of the starch from the rice thus shaving off some calories from this dish.

Tip: The drained out water can act as an excellent stock for soups especially when it comes out of the local red coloured rice.

Prep time: 20 minutes

Cooking time: 10 minutes with a pressure cooker; 15-20 minutes with a deep pan

Total time: 30 minutes with a pressure cooker; 35-40 minutes with a deep pan

Curd Rice

This is a very simple, light and delicious dish to have in hot summers. This is a perennial favourite all over Southern India, where many prefer ending their meals NOT with a dessert but with curd rice!

Ingredients

Cooked rice-2 cups

Yoghurt-1 cup

Clarified butter (*Ghee*)-1 tablespoon

Black Mustard-1/2 teaspoon

Ginger-1/2 inch piece chopped up finely

Curry leaves-a few

Roasted *Channa dal* (roasted split chick peas)-1/2 teaspoon

Salt to taste

Optional: You can also add finely sliced carrots and deseeded, chopped green chillies for flavour if you so desire.

Method

In a bowl, mix together the yoghurt, rice and salt.

In a small tempering pan, add the clarified butter (*Ghee*) and put it on your heat source.

As soon as the clarified butter warms up, add the black mustard seeds, ginger, *channa* dal (split chick peas) and the curry leaves and let them all splutter and sizzle.

If adding carrot and green chillies, add it to the tempering pan at this point. Let the carrots cook a little.

Add to the rice and yoghurt mixture.

Your curd rice is ready.

Prep time: 5 minutes

Cooking time: 2 minutes

Total time: 7 minutes

Lemon rice

This delicious twist on cooked rice too is a favourite dish in South India.

Ingredients

Cooked rice-2 cups

Lemon juice-2 tablespoon

Clarified butter (*Ghee*) -1 tablespoon

Black Mustard-1/2 teaspoon

Ginger-1/2 inch piece chopped up finely

Curry leaves-a few

Deseeded chopped green chillies-1/2 teaspoon (this is only for flavour and not to make it hot)

Turmeric-1/2 teaspoon

Asafoetida (*Hing*)-a pinch

Roasted *Channa* dal (roasted split chick peas)-1/2 teaspoon

Water-2 tablespoon

Salt to taste

Method

In a small wok, add the clarified butter (*Ghee*) and put it on your heat source.

As soon as the clarified butter warms up, add the black mustard seeds, ginger, *channa* dal (split chick peas) and the curry leaves till they all splutter and sizzle.

Now add the green chillies, turmeric and asafoetida.

Add the rice, water and salt. Mix well.

Turn off your heat source and add the lemon juice.

Again Mix well.

Your lemon rice is ready.

Prep time: 5 minutes

Cooking time: 2 minutes

Total time: 7 minutes

Onion Rice

This is the poor man's *pulao* made in a Jiffy. You can use this recipe to add some zing to your left over rice, the North Indian way.

Ingredients

Cooked rice-2 cups

Onion sliced- 2 medium size

Cumin seeds (*Jeera*)-1/2 teaspoon

Green Cardamom (*Chhoti elaichi*)-2

Cinnamon (*Dalchini*)-1/2 inch

Cloves (*Laung*)-4

Bay leaf (*Tejpatta*)-1

Clarified butter (*Ghee*)-1 tablespoon

Salt to taste

Sugar-1/4 teaspoon (dissolved in 2 tablespoon water)

Method

Place a small wok on your heat source.

Add the clarified butter (*Ghee*).

When the butter warms up, add the cumin seeds along with the cardamom, cinnamon, cloves and bay leaves. Stir a little.

As soon as it starts giving off a nice aroma, in less than a minute, add the onion slices. Do please make sure that the spices brown and not burn, otherwise your dish will be totally spoiled.

Fry till the onions become nicely golden brown.

Add the rice. Mix well.

Now, add the salt and the sugar which has already been dissolved in water. Stir again to mix well.

Switch off the heat source and take out the rice. Enjoy!!!

Prep time: 5 minutes

Cooking time: 2 minutes

Total time: 7 minutes

Jeera Pulao (Cumin Rice)

This is how the basic Indian *pulao* is made. If you master this, you can make any kind of *pulao*.

Ingredients

Long grain rice (Basmati)-1 cup

Water-2 cups

Cumin seeds (*Jeera*)-1/2 teaspoon

Green Cardamom (*Chhoti elaichi*)-2

Cinnamon (*Dalchini*)-1/2 inch

Cloves (*Laung*)-4

Bay leaf (*Tejpatta*)-1

Clarified butter (*Ghee*)-1 tablespoon

Salt to taste

Sugar-1/4 teaspoon

Method

Wash the rice well (*in a vessel 3-4 times, but don't rub it lest the grains break*) and let it naturally "dry", on an inclined plate, for 15-20 minutes. This helps enhance the aroma.

If using a pressure cooker

In a pressure cooker, add the clarified butter and place it on your heat source.

When the butter warms up, add the cumin seeds along with the cardamom, cinnamon, cloves and bay leaves.

As soon as it starts giving a nice aroma, in less than a minute, add the rice along with the salt and sugar. Do please make sure that the spices brown and not burn, otherwise your dish will be totally spoiled.

Stir well.

Add the water.

Close the lid of the pressure cooker BUT remove the *weight*.

When steam starts escaping from the vent (*don't worry, you will hear that typical sound*), reduce the heat to minimum. In other words, if cooking on gas, turn the knob to SIM (mer).

Wait for 10 minutes and switch off the gas. Take out the rice.

Your hot fluffy *Jeera Pulao* is ready.

If using a thick bottomed pan/vessel

In a pan/vessel, add the clarified butter and place on fire.

When the butter warms up, add the cumin seeds along with the cardamom, cinnamon, cloves and bay leaves.

As soon as it starts giving a nice aroma in less than a minute, add the rice along with the salt and sugar. Do please make sure that the spices brown and not burn, otherwise your dish will be totally spoiled.

Stir well.

Add the water.

Cover the pan/vessel with a well-fitting lid.

Reduce the heat to minimum. In other words, if cooking on gas, turn the knob to SIM (mer). Let the rice cook for 15-20 minutes.

Switch off the heat source and let the rice remain in the vessel for another 5 minutes. Take out the rice.

Your hot fluffy *Jeera Pulao* is ready.

Prep time: 20 minutes

Cooking time: 12 minutes with a pressure cooker; 17-22 minutes with a deep pan

Total time: 32 minutes with a pressure cooker; 37-42 minutes with a deep pan

Mattar Pulao (Peas Rice)

Ingredients

Long grain rice (Basmati)-1 cup

Peas-1/2 cup

Sliced Onion-1 (Medium)

Water-2 cups

Cumin seeds (*Jeera*)-1/2 teaspoon

Green Cardamom (*Chhoti elaichi*)-2

Cinnamon (*Dalchini*)-1/2 inch

Cloves (*Laung*)-4

Bay leaf (*Tejpatta*)-1

Clarified butter (*Ghee*)-2 tablespoon

Salt to taste

Sugar-1/4 teaspoon

Method

Wash the rice well (*in a vessel 3-4 times, but don't rub it lest the grains break*) and let it naturally "dry", on an inclined plate, for 15-20 minutes. This helps enhance the aroma.

If using a pressure cooker

In a pressure cooker, add the clarified butter and place it on your heat source.

When the butter warms up, add the cumin seeds along with the cardamom, cinnamon, cloves and bay leaves.

As soon as it starts giving a nice aroma, in less than a minute, add the onion slices and fry till translucent. Do please make sure that the spices brown and not burn, otherwise your dish will be totally spoiled.

Add the peas and stir for a minute.

Now add the rice along with the salt and sugar.

Stir well.

Add the water.

Close the lid of the pressure cooker BUT remove the *weight*.

When steam starts escaping from the vent (*don't worry, you will hear that typical sound*), reduce the heat to minimum. In other words, if cooking on gas, turn the knob to SIM (mer).

Wait for 10 minutes and switch off the gas.

Take out the rice. Your *pea pulao* is ready.

If using a thick bottomed pan/vessel

In a pan/vessel, add the clarified butter and place on fire.

When the butter warms up, add the cumin seeds along with the cardamom, cinnamon, cloves and bay leaves.

As soon as it starts giving a nice aroma, in less than a minute, add the onion slices and fry till translucent. Do please make sure that the spices brown and not burn, otherwise your dish will be totally spoiled.

Add the peas and stir for a minute. Now add the rice along with the salt and sugar. Stir well. Add the water. Cover the pan/vessel with a well-fitting lid.

Reduce the heat to minimum. In other words, if cooking on gas, turn the knob to SIM (mer). Let the rice cook for 15-20 minutes.

Switch off the heat source and let the rice remain in the vessel for another 5 minutes. Take out the rice. Your *pea pulao* is ready.

Prep time: 20 minutes

Cooking time: 12 minutes with a pressure cooker; 17-22 minutes with a deep pan

Total time: 32 minutes with a pressure cooker; 37-42 minutes with a deep pan

Khichdi (Mixture of Rice, Lentil and Veggie Dish)

Khichdi literally means a mixture. In some form or another, this is almost compulsorily prepared for the festival of *Makar Sakranti* that is celebrated all over India and Nepal. This festival is also known as *Pongal* in Tamil Nadu, *Bihu* in Assam, *Lohri* in Punjab or *Uttarayan* in Gujarat.

Interestingly, this is one of the few Hindu festivals that falls on the fixed day of 14 January, when the Sun moves from the Tropic of Capricorn to the Tropic of Cancer heralding the arrival of spring and the beginning of the harvest season.

It is believed that on this day, Lord *Surya* (the Sun God) visits the house of his son *Shani* (Saturn), who is the lord of the *Makar rashi* (Capricorn) and the controller of the quantum of misfortune befalling humans. To appease *Shani*, therefore, many Indians prefer cooking *Khichdi* on Saturdays which is also known as *Shaniwar* or the day of Lord *Shani*.

Khichdi is otherwise the most nutritiously complete dish, consisting of carbs from rice, proteins from lentils and vitamins from veggies. Also it is quite a JIFFY dish.

Ingredients

Rice-3/4 glass

Moong Dal (Bengal Gram)-1/4 glass

Onion-1 (chopped up)

Ginger-1 inch

Spinach (only leaves)-500 grams or 18oz coarsely chopped

Peas--100 grams (3.5oz)

Carrots-2 (cut into small pieces)

Tomato-1

Khada (that is, whole and not powdered) *Garam Masala* (Green cardamom--2, brown cardamom-1, Bay leaves-2, cinnamon stick-1/2 inch, black pepper-6, cloves-4, cumin seeds-1/2 tea spoon)

Coriander (*Dhania*) powder-1 teaspoon

Red chilli powder (only for flavour and not to make it hot)-1/4 teaspoon (you can add more if you like it hot)

Turmeric (*Haldi*)-1 teaspoon

Asafoetida (*Hing*)-1/4 teaspoon

Ghee (clarified butter)-2 tablespoon full

Salt- 1 level teaspoon roughly or to taste.

Water-3 glasses (This will give your *Khichdi* a wet consistency. However, if you like your *khichdi* to be drier, then add only 2 glasses of water instead of 3.)

Method

Wash the rice and dal together and let it dry for 5 minutes on an inclined plate.

If using a pressure cooker

In a pressure cooker, put the clarified butter and put it on your heat source.

As it warms up, add the *Khada Garam Masala* and Asafoetida.

Let these all crackle but NOT burn.

Add the onion and ginger.

Sauté this for 2 minutes and then add the peas and the carrots.

Stir well.

Now add the coarsely chopped spinach, turmeric, coriander powder, red chilli powder and salt.

Add the rice, dal and the tomatoes.

Stir well.

Add the water and put the lid with the weight on the cooker.

After the cooker comes to full pressure, switch off the heat source but do NOT release the pressure.

Let the pressure cooker cool down by itself.

Open the cooker and you will find your *Khichdi* ready.

If using a thick bottomed pan/vessel

In a pan/vessel, add the clarified butter and place it on your heat source.

When the butter warms up, add the *Khada Garam Masala* and Asafoetida (*Hing*).

Let these all crackle but NOT burn.

Add the onion and ginger.

Sauté this for 2 minutes.

Then add the peas and the carrots.

Stir well.

Then add the coarsely chopped spinach, turmeric, coriander powder, red chilli powder and salt.

Add the rice, dal and the tomatoes.

Stir well.

Add the water.

Cover the pan/vessel with a well-fitting lid.

Reduce the heat to minimum. In other words, if cooking on gas, turn the knob to SIM (mer). Let the *Khichdi* cook for 15-20 minutes.

Switch off the heat source and let the rice remain in the vessel for another 5 minutes.

Your *Khichdi* should now be ready.

Prep time: 5 minutes

Cooking time: 10 minutes with a pressure cooker; 20-25 minutes with a deep pan

Total time: 15 minutes with a pressure cooker; 25-30 minutes with a deep pan

Breads

The Classic Indian Roti/Phulka/Chapati

This simple Indian bread, free of yeast or any other leavening agent, is what many Indian homes have every day for lunch or dinner. It is surprising then that most restaurants don't have *chapatis* on their menus. Instead they focus on making *Tandoori Rotis* or *Nans*, which they probably find easier to handle when larger numbers are to be served.

For most households, however, it won't be easy to invest in a *Tandoor* (earthen oven). For them then it will have to be the simple, non-fussy *Chapati*. And here's how you can go about making these.

Note: I have seen people rolling dough with a steel tumbler on any flat surface, or using just their hands to give dough the roundish shape of a roti. I think it prudent, however, for all newbies to invest in a rolling pin (*belan*) and rolling board (*chakla*) before attempting to make *chapatis*.

Ingredients

Whole Wheat Flour-3 cups (enough for 5 *chapatis*)

Luke Warm Water-1 cup

Method

In a mixing bowl, put 2 + ½ cups of flour, reserving ½ cup as *parthan* (dusting) for rolling out the *chapatis* later.

Add the water and make into a nice firm dough.

Shape the dough into balls about the size of a large walnut.

In another plate, put the remaining wheat flour (the reserved ½ cup), and press the ball into this dry flour.

At this point, take a thick griddle and put it on your heat source.

While the griddle heats up, take out your rolling board (*Chakla).*

Using a rolling pin (*Belan*), shape the dough ball (that is already rolled into the dry flour), into a small circular shape as thin as you can make it.

Now, on the heated griddle place this rolled out *chapati.*

Let it cook a little on one side and then flip over for the other side to also cook.

Using a tong, remove the *chapati* from the griddle and place it directly on the flame.

The *chapati* will immediately swell up and will be ready to be served.

In case you don't have a heat source with a flame, then you will have to puff up the *chapati* on the griddle itself. For this you will need a handkerchief with which you should gently press the edges of the *chapati* as it swells on the griddle flipping it for a second time.

Prep time: 5 minutes

Cooking time: 5 minutes for 5 *chapatis* @1 minute per *chapati*

Total time: 10 minutes

Pooris

This magical version of the humble *chapati* is an eternal favourite of both households as well as restaurants. Because this is fried, it has a longer shelf life than *chapatis* and tastes better too. This is why *pooris* are very popular for picnics, outings and as *prasadam* (blessings) in many Hindu temples.

Ingredients

Whole Wheat Flour-3 cups (enough for 12 *pooris*)

Salt-1/2 teaspoon

Cooking Oil-1 tablespoonful

Luke Warm Water-1 cup

Cooking Oil/Clarified Butter (*Ghee*) for deep frying; *Ghee* is preferred if you want the authentic taste.

Method

In a mixing bowl, mix together the wheat flour, salt and one tablespoon cooking oil.

Now make a firm dough by adding the water. Cover the dough and leave it for ½ an hour.

Before rolling out *Pooris*, it is advisable to knead the dough once again.

Make small balls, smaller than for *Chapatis*, and roll out on a rolling board (*Chakla*) with a rolling pin (*Belan*).

Tip: Remember your *Pooris* are going into hot oil. You should not, therefore, dust it with any dry flour, as you did in the case of the *chapatis*, as this will make your frying oil dirtier. So later, if you use this oil for frying more *Pooris*, they will inevitably acquire a more bitter taste because of the burnt flour dust accumulating inside.

In a small wok, add the cooking oil (or *Ghee*) till it is ½ full. Heat the oil till a faint haze arises from the oil.

Now, place the rolled out *Pooris* one by one into this hot oil. Gently turn with a slotted spoon and gently press the *Pooris* till they swell up magically like a balloon. Remove the *Pooris* from the oil and put it on a plate covered with a paper napkin so that excess oil is absorbed.

Enjoy the delicious *Pooris* with any vegetable, meat or even sweet dish like *kheer* or *halwa*.

Tip: The oil or *Ghee* used for *Pooris* should be stored in a fridge and used up for other dishes as soon as possible.

Prep time: 35 minutes

Cooking time: 8 minutes for 12 *pooris* @40 seconds per *Poori*

Total time: 43 minutes

Classic Varki Paratha

Yet another and really delicious version of the Indian unleavened bread, *parathas* are very popular for breakfasts, picnics and tours. Because these too are fried, somewhat more lightly than *pooris*, they do have a longer shelf life than *chapatis*.

Compared to *pooris, parathas* are much more amenable to all kinds of fillings. You also require much less cooking oil/*Ghee* to cook *parathas*, which makes these the favourite of all economically conscious households as well as restaurants.

Here's then the recipe for the classic *varki paratha*, where *varki* means you can peel the *parathas* quite magically layer by layer.

Ingredients

Whole Wheat Flour-3 cups (enough for 5 *parathas*)

Salt-1/2 teaspoon

Cooking Oil-1 tablespoonful

Luke Warm Water-1 cup

Cooking Oil or Clarified Butter (*Ghee*) for roasting the *Parathas*; *Ghee* is preferred if you want the authentic taste.

Method

In a mixing bowl, mix together the wheat flour, salt and one tablespoon cooking oil.

Now make a firm dough by adding the water. Cover the dough and leave for ½ an hour.

Take a large walnut sized dough and roll into a ball.

Now, flatten it on the rolling board as in the case of *Chapatis*.

When the dough is thin and round, spread a few drops of cooking oil on the surface and fold it in half. Spread a few more drops of cooking oil on this half and again fold to make a triangle.

Now, on the rolling board (*chakla*) and with a rolling pin (*Belan*), gently stretch this triangle to the biggest triangle you can manage or to the original size of the round *Chapati*.

Put a griddle on your heat source.

As soon as the griddle becomes hot, place the *Paratha* on it.

Reduce the flame to medium and let the *Paratha* cook on one side.

Flip over and let it cook on the other side.

Take a teaspoon of oil/*Ghee* and cover the side facing you with that.

Flip over and repeat the process till the *Paratha* gets a nice, crisp texture.

Line a casserole with a paper napkin and place the *Paratha* inside it to keep it hot.

Repeat the process till all the *Parathas* are made.

Enjoy your hot *Parathas* with any vegetables or meat dish.

Prep time: 35 minutes

Cooking time: 5 minutes for 5 *parathas* @1 minute per *parathas*

Total time: 40 minutes

CHAPTER 6

DALS (LENTILS)

Call them soups or curries, but you will find *dals* in every home in India. They may be spiced or tempered in as many ways as there are regions and languages in India. But the common thread would be that, as sources of excellent vegetarian protein, they should be on every Indian's platter.

A word of warning though. Most *dals* necessitate the use of pressure cookers if you want to cook them in a jiffy. However, if you do not have a pressure cooker, you can still cook *dals* in deep sauce pans. This is how most of rural India and wayside eateries still cook their lentils, but that does take a much, much longer time. You will also need to check the *dals* once in a while, while they are cooking, to see whether they have become soft and cooked to your liking.

Tip: Pre-soaking some *dals* overnight will help reduce their cooking time.

I shall now present the ten most popular "Home Style" dal recipes, using *Arhar/Toor Dal* (Split Pigeon Peas), *Chana Dal* (Split Chick Pea), *Masoor Dal* (Red Lentils), *Moong Dal* (Bengal Gram), *Chhola* (Whole Chick Pea), and *Rajma* (Red Kidney Beans).

Arhar Dal (Split Pigeon Peas)

Ingredients

Arhar/Toor (split pigeon peas) Dal-1/2 Small cup

Water-4 small cups (same cup as above!)

Turmeric (*Haldi)* powder-1/2 tea spoon

Salt--1/2 tea spoon or to taste

Tomato--1

Cumin seeds (*Jeera*) -- 1/2   tea spoon

Ghee (clarified butter)-1 tea spoon

Fresh Coriander leaves (optional)

Method

Wash the *Arhar Dal* (same style as for rice) and put it in the pressure cooker with water, *haldi*, salt, and chopped tomato.

Close the lid with *weight* (unlike rice), put it on your heat source and let it come to full pressure (i.e. *when the weight lifts and there is a whistling sound*).

Thereafter reduce the heat to minimum (to Sim on a gas stove) and let it cook for 5 more minutes.

Turn the gas off and let the cooker cool down.

Take a tempering pan and add the *ghee*.

When it warms up, add the cumin seeds and let these splutter. Please ensure that the cumin doesn't burn and only turns brown.

Add this to the dal.

Your simple *Arhar Dal* is ready.

If you want, you may add some chopped fresh coriander leaves and serve.

Prep time: 5 minutes for washing and collecting all ingredients

Cooking time: 12 minutes for cooking with pressure cooker.

Total time: 17 minutes

Arhar Dal (Variation with rai, onion, garlic and curry leaves)

The western Indian states of Gujarat and Maharashtra prefer to cook their *Arhar/Toor dal* with this tasty twist, where they use *Rai* and curry leaves in place of *Jeera* and coriander leaves. Do try this out.

Ingredients

Arhar/Toor (split pigeon peas) Dal-1/2 Small cup

Water-4 small cups (same cup as above!)

Turmeric (*Haldi*) powder-1/2 tea spoon

Salt--1/2 tea spoon or to taste

Tomato--2

Onion-1

Garlic-4 pieces

Rai (Black Mustard seed whole) -- 1/2   tea spoon

Curry leaves-few

Ghee (clarified butter)-2 tea spoon

Method

Wash the *Arhar Dal* and put it in the pressure cooker with water, *haldi*, salt, and chopped tomatoes, onion and garlic.

Close the lid with weight, put it on your heat source and let it come to full pressure (i.e. *when the weight lifts and there is a whistling sound*).

Thereafter reduce the heat to minimum (to Sim on a gas stove) and let it cook for 5 more minutes.

Turn the heat source off and let the cooker cool down.

Take a tempering pan and add the *ghee*.

When it warms up, add the *rai* till it splutters and then add the curry leaves.

Please ensure that the *rai* doesn't burn.

Add this to the *dal*.

Your simple *Arhar Dal* variation is ready.

Prep time: 5 minutes for washing and collecting all ingredients

Cooking time: 12 minutes for cooking with pressure cooker

Total time: 17 minutes

Chana Dal (Split Chick Pea)

This is one of those rare lentils which is cooked with *garam masala*. This makes it go well with *Pulao* or even meat dishes that are cooked with *garam masala*.

Ingredients

Chana Dal (split chick pea)-1/2 cup

Water-4 cups (same cup as above!)

Turmeric (*Haldi*) powder-1/2 tea spoon

Salt--1/2 tea spoon or to taste

Tomato--2

Onion-1

Garlic-2 pieces

Ginger-1 inch

Cumin seeds (*Jeera*) -- 1/2   tea spoon

Garam Masala (mixture of common Indian spices) crushed -1/2   tea spoon

Ghee (clarified butter)-2 tea spoon

Method

Wash the *Chana Dal*.

Put the pressure cooker on your heat source and add *ghee* (Clarified butter).

When the *ghee* heats up, add the cumin seeds for browning.

Add the chopped up onion, garlic and ginger. Sauté for 2 minutes.

Add the tomatoes and sauté for another minute.

Add the dal, turmeric, salt, and water and *garam masala*.

Close the lid and let it come to full pressure.

Reduce heat (to Sim on a gas stove) and let it cook for 10 more minutes.

Turn off the heat source and let the cooker cool down.

Your simple *Chana dal* is ready.

Prep time: 5 minutes for washing and collecting all ingredients

Cooking time: 15 minutes with pressure cooker

Total time: 20 minutes

Masoor Dal (Whole Red Lentils)

Ingredients

Whole *Masoor* Dal-1/2 cup

Water-4 cups (same cup as above!)

Turmeric (*Haldi*) powder-1/2 tea spoon

Salt--1/2 tea spoon or to taste

Tomato--2

Onion-1

Garlic-2 pieces

Cumin seeds (*Jeera*) -- 1/2   tea spoon

Ghee (clarified butter)-2 tea spoon

Method

Wash the *Masoor* Dal.

Put the cooker on your heat source and add *ghee* (Clarified butter).

When the *ghee* heats up, add the cumin seeds for browning.

Add the chopped up onion and garlic.

Sauté for 2 minutes.

Add the tomatoes and sauté some more for another minute.

Add the *dal*, turmeric, salt and water.

Close the lid and let it come to full pressure.

Reduce the heat (to SIM on a gas stove) and let it cook for 10 minutes.

Turn off the heat source and let the cooker cool down.

Your simple *Masoor* dal is ready.

Prep time: 5 minutes for washing and collecting all ingredients

Cooking time: 13 minutes with pressure cooker

Total time: 18 minutes

Dhuli Masoor Dal (Split Red Lentils)

Ingredients

Dhuli Masoor (split red lentils) Dal-1/2 cup

Water-4 cups

Turmeric (*Haldi)* powder-1/2 teaspoon

Salt--1/2 teaspoon or to taste

Tomato--2

Cumin seeds (*Jeera*) -- 1/2   tea spoon

Garlic-4 cloves

Whole Red Chilli-1

Cooking Oil-1 tea spoon

Fresh Coriander (optional)

Method

Wash the *Masoor Dal* and put it in the pressure cooker with water, *haldi*, salt, and chopped tomato.

Close the lid with weight, put it on your heat source and let it come to full pressure (i.e. *when the weight lifts and there is a whistling sound*).

Thereafter switch off the heat source and let the cooker cool down.

Take a tempering pan and add the cooking oil.

When it warms up, add the cumin seeds and whole red chilli and let it splutter. Please ensure that the cumin doesn't burn and only turns brown.

Add the garlic and let it roast for a few seconds till it starts giving off a lovely aroma.

Add this to the *dal*.

Your simple *Dhuli Masoor Dal* is ready.

If you want, you may add some chopped fresh coriander leaves to it and serve.

Prep time: 5 minutes for washing and collecting all ingredients

Cooking time: 7 minutes with pressure cooker

Total time: 12 minutes

Dhuli Moong Dal (Split Bengal gram)

Ingredients

Dhuli Moong (split Bengal gram) Dal-1/2 cup

Water-4 cups (same cup as above!)

Turmeric (*Haldi*) powder-1/2 tea spoon

Salt--1/2 tea spoon or to taste

Tomato--1

Cumin seeds (*Jeera*) -- 1/2   tea spoon

Ghee (clarified butter)-1 tea spoon

Fresh Coriander (optional)

Method

Wash the *Moong Dal* and put it in the pressure cooker with water, *haldi*, salt, and chopped tomato.

Close the lid with weight, put it on your heat source and let it come to full pressure (i.e. *when the weight lifts and there is a whistling sound*).

Thereafter switch off the heat source and let the cooker cool down.

Take a tempering pan and add the ghee.

When it warms up, add the cumin and let it splutter.

Please ensure that the cumin doesn't burn and only turns brown.

Add this to the *dal*.

Your simple *Moong Dal* is ready.

If you want, you may add some chopped fresh coriander leaves to it and serve.

Prep time: 5 minutes for washing and collecting all ingredients

Cooking time: 7 minutes with pressure cooker

Total time: 12 minutes

Sambar

The South Indian states of Andhra Pradesh, Tamil Nadu, Karnataka and Kerala prefer to cook their *Arhar/Toor dal* with this fiery but tasty twist. In fact, they love *Sambar* so much that they have to have it for all meals--breakfast, lunch and dinner!

Be careful, this is NOT a mild lentil soup.

Ingredients

Arhar/Toor (split pigeon peas) *Dal*-1 small cup

Water-4 cups (same cup as above!)

Onion-1

Tomatoes-2

Garlic-6 cloves

Beans-100 grams (3.5oz)

Pumpkin-100 grams (3.5oz)

Bottle Gourd-100 grams (3.5oz)

Sambar masala powder-4 teaspoon

Tamarind paste-1 tablespoon dissolved in 1/2 cup of water

Ghee-1 tablespoon

Black Mustard seeds (*Rai*)-1 teaspoon

Curry leaves-10-12

Salt to taste

Sugar-1/2 teaspoon

Method

Wash the *dal* and vegetables well. Chop up the vegetables, onion, tomatoes and garlic.

In a pressure cooker, put the dal and the chopped vegetables along with the chopped onion, tomatoes and garlic.

Add the *sambar masala*, salt and sugar.

Add water.

Close the lid and put it on your heat source.

When the pressure cooker comes to full pressure, reduce the heat (to SIM on a gas stove) and let it cook for 7 minutes.

Let the cooker cool down on its own and then open it.

Add the tamarind paste and boil it once more without covering it with the lid.

In a tempering pan, add the ghee, the black mustard seeds and the curry leaves and let it splutter.

Add this to the *Sambar*. Your *Sambar* is ready.

In case, you cannot get curry leaves, black mustard seeds alone can also impart the required flavour.

If you like your *Sambar* to taste more sour, you can add more tamarind paste. Similarly, if you want your *Sambar* to taste sweeter, you can add more sugar.

Prep time: 8 minutes for washing, chopping and collecting all ingredients

Cooking time: 12 minutes with pressure cooker

Total time: 20 minutes

Rajma (Red Kidney Beans curry)

A perennial favourite of the North Indian states of Punjab, Haryana, Himachal Pradesh and Jammu & Kashmir, this dish is cooked more like meat than lentils. Many wayside eateries or *dhabas* thrive on serving just *Rajma* with fragrant Basmati rice and readily find a seemingly never ending queue of diners.

Try this dish once and you will not touch that insipid Baked Beans with tomato sauce can ever again.

Ingredients

Red Kidney beans (*Rajma*)-1 small cup

Water-4 cups (same cup as above!)

Chopped Onion-1

Chopped Garlic-5 cloves

Chopped Ginger-1 inch

Chopped Tomatoes-4

Garam Masala powder-1/2 teaspoon

Turmeric (*Haldi*)-1/2 teaspoon

Cumin seeds (*Jeera*)-1/2 teaspoon

Kashmiri red chilli powder-1/2 teaspoon (just for flavour and not to make it hot)

Clarified butter (*Ghee*)-2 tablespoon

Salt to taste

Sugar-1/4 teaspoon

Method

Soak the kidney beans overnight in 2 cups of water.

Note: Remember if you don't pre-soak the beans, the cooking time will be extremely long and the beans may not cook that easily.

Place the pressure cooker on your heat source.

Add the clarified butter and when it melts, add the cumin seeds.

As soon as the cumin seeds turn brown, which takes just a few seconds (Do please make sure they don't burn), add the chopped onion, garlic and ginger.

Sauté well till the onions become translucent and start giving a nice aroma.

Add the kidney beans, along with the chilli powder, turmeric powder, *garam masala*, salt and sugar.

Sauté for about a minute.

To this mixture, now add the tomatoes.

Roast well till the tomatoes are cooked.

Now add 4 cups of water and close the lid.

Let the cooker come to full pressure i.e. when steam starts escaping from the vent (*don't worry, you will hear that typical sound*), and then immediately reduce the heat to minimum. In other words, if cooking on gas, turn the knob to SIM (mer).

Cook on low heat for 15 minutes more.

Thereafter turn off the heat source and let the cooker cool on its own.

Open the lid and see if the *Rajma* has the desired consistency. In case you want it to be more wettish, you can add some more water. In case you want it drier, then you can put it back on the heat source without the lid and let the water evaporate. While doing either, please remember to keep stirring, so that the *Rajma* does not get burnt.

This dish tastes delicious with plain, long grain Basmati rice.

Prep time: Soak overnight. After that prep time should be about 5 minutes for washing and collecting all ingredients.

Cooking time: 20 minutes with pressure cooker

Total time: 25 minutes

Chhola (Whole Chick Pea Curry)

This is another classic dish of the North Indian states of Punjab, Haryana, Himachal Pradesh and Jammu & Kashmir. Again, like *Rajma*, this dish too is cooked more like meat than lentils. However, unlike *Rajma* which is traditionally enjoyed with fragrant Basmati rice, *Chhola* is paired more with *Pooris* (fried and puffed up Indian unleavened bread) and *Bhathuras* (fried and puffed up Indian leavened bread). This combo is in fact quite a favourite for breakfasts or rather brunches.

Try this dish with rice or any kind of bread, western or Indian, and I bet you will fall in love with it.

Ingredients

Whole white chick pea (*Kabuli Chana or Chhola*)-1 small cup

Onions-2

Garlic-6 cloves

Ginger-1+1/2 inches

Tomatoes-3

Cumin seeds (*Jeera*)-1/2 teaspoon

Coriander powder-2 teaspoon

Turmeric- 1 teaspoon

Garam Masala powder-1/2 teaspoon

Kashmiri Red Chilli powder-1/2 teaspoon

Cooking Oil- 2 tablespoon

Salt to taste

Method

Soak the chick pea in a vessel with water (which covers the chick peas completely) at least for 4 hours. This way when you cook the chick peas, they become nice and tender and take less time to cook.

Put the pre-soaked chick peas in a pressure cooker, with enough water to cover the chick peas.

Switch on the heat source and close the lid of the pressure cooker with weight.

When the cooker comes to full pressure, reduce the heat (to Sim on a gas stove) and let the chick peas cook for 10 minutes more.

Turn off the heat source and let the cooker cool down.

In a grinder, make a fine paste of the tomatoes, ginger, garlic and onion.

Place a wok on a heat source and add the cooking oil.

When the oil warms up, add the cumin seeds.

In a few seconds, as soon as the cumin seeds turn brown, add the paste you have just made in the grinder. Do please ensure that the cumin seeds do not burn.

Sauté the paste till it starts giving a nice aroma.

Now add the turmeric powder, *garam masala*, red chilli powder and coriander powder.

Sauté for another 2 minutes.

Now, add the chick peas (without the water) to this mixture.

Mix well and add the salt.

Then, add as much water as you like depending upon the thickness of the curry that you want.

Let the mixture boil for about 2 minutes so that all the ingredients are well blended.

Your *Chhola* is ready.

Prep time: Soak overnight or at least for 4 hours. After that prep time should be 5 minutes for washing and collecting all ingredients.

Cooking time: 20 minutes with pressure cooker

Total time: 25 minutes

Note: If you have sampled *Chhola* in a *dhaba*, you may find my "Home Style" recipe a little mild. This is for two main reasons. First, since the *dhabas* have to cook huge quantities (say 10 Kgs or 22 lbs of Chick Peas in one go), and that too in big non-pressurised vessels, they slip in some baking soda to their pre-soaking process. I'm not in favour of this practice because this unnecessarily increases the sodium levels of your *Chhola* (which is bad for your blood pressure) without enhancing the taste. In fact, the somewhat soapy taste that baking soda imparts to this dish may not suit sensitive palates.

Which leads to the second point, of drowning this baking soda induced flavour. This is done by using stronger spices like *Kastoori Methi* (fragrant Fenugreek). Then *Anardana* (ground seeds of wild pomegranate) is used to increase the tanginess of the dish. Finally, used tea leaves are added to impart a blackish colour to the *Chhola*.

I have nothing against the second point. Use this if you crave the authentic *dhaba* flavour.

But for the first, you may be better off using a pressure cooker or a slow cooker than using baking soda.

Karhi (Yoghurt chickpea flour curry)

This dish was probably invented for those days when you couldn't get any fresh green vegetables in the local village market. That need has more or less disappeared with the arrival of supermarkets that access food from anywhere in the world.

Nonetheless, *Karhi* remains quite popular not only in Northern India but in Western India also, with a little variation.

Here is the Western Indian version, which I find tastier.

Ingredients

Plain Yoghurt-1 cup

Chickpea flour (*Besan*)-2 tablespoon

Turmeric powder (*Haldi*)-1 teaspoon

Coriander powder-1 teaspoon

Kashmiri Red Chilli powder- ½ teaspoon (just for flavour)

Sugar- 1 teaspoon

Ground Asafoetida (*Hing*)-1/4 teaspoon

Whole green chilli-1 (just for flavour. If you like your *karhi* to be hot, then you can chop the green chilli in small pieces and mix it.)

Salt-1 teaspoon or to taste

Water-2 + ½ cups

Clarified butter (*Ghee*) - 1 teaspoon

Black Mustard seeds (*Rai*)-1/2 teaspoon

Curry leaves-few

Method

In a wok, mix together the yoghurt, Chickpea flour (*Besan*), Turmeric powder (*Haldi*), Coriander powder, *Kashmiri Red Chilli* powder, Sugar, Asafoetida (*Hing*), Whole green chilli, and salt.

Mix well and then add the water.

Switch on the heat source and place the wok on it.

Let the mixture come to a boil and keep stirring till it gets a nice slightly thick consistency (approximately 5 minutes).

Remove thereafter from the heat source.

Separately, in a tempering pan, add the clarified butter, the black mustard seeds and the curry leaves.

As soon as the mustard seeds (*rai*) splutter, turn off the heat source and add the entire contents of the tempering pan to the *Karhi* in the wok.

This *Karhi* tastes really good with rice.

You can also add *Pakoris* (vegetables rolled in *besan* and fried) to the *Karhi*.

If you prefer the North Indian version of *Karhi*, then leave out the curry leaves and *Rai* from the above recipe.

Prep time: 5 minutes

Cooking time: 7 minutes

Total time: 12 minutes

CHAPTER 7

VEGETABLE DISHES

No one cooks vegetables as well and in as many ways as the Indians do. Broadly, there appear to be three distinct ways of cooking veggies. First, the North Indian way that uses *Garam Masala*. Second, the East Indian way that uses *Pachphoran*, a mixture of five other spices that don't constitute *garam masala*. And then, there is the South Indian version that prefers neither *garam masala* nor *pachforan* but uses a totally different way of making veggies by using black mustard seeds, curry leaves, and coconut.

All three versions are absolutely mouth-watering. I am sure you can't say the same about most of the Western or even Oriental vegetable dishes, which to the Indian palate tastes like "salad", unless you use chicken stock or fish sauce to impart some taste or flavour. But then, that won't make them "pure vegetarian", would they?

With this strong introduction, I now present 15 recipes; five North Indian, four South Indian, five Eastern Indian, and one special quickie for my Western friends.

Let me start with the North Indian school version first.

Band Gobi, Gaajar, Aloo, Mattar Sabzi (Cabbage, Carrot, Potatoes and Peas Curry)

Ingredients

Cabbage--1/2 Kg (500 grams or 18oz)

Green peas (shelled, fresh are preferred) --200 grams (7oz)

Potatoes-2

Carrot--2

Medium size Onions--2

Garlic-4 pieces

Ginger-1 inch

Fresh tomato-2

Turmeric (*Haldi*) - 1/2 tea spoon

Dry crushed coriander-2 tea spoon

Garam Masala (mixture of common Indian spices) crushed- 1/2 tea spoon

Kashmiri Red Chilli powder--1/4 tea spoon (Recommended for colour, but if you like your dish to be really spicy, use some other red chilli powder)

Cumin (*Jeera*) whole-1/2 tea spoon

Salt-1 level tea spoon (or to taste)

Tomato Ketchup-1 table spoon

Cooking oil-1 table spoon

Ghee (clarified butter)-1 tea spoon

Water-1 tea cup

Method

Blend together (in a blender preferably!) the onions, garlic, ginger and tomatoes to a fine paste.

Heat the oil in a pressure cooker. (In case you don't have a pressure cooker, you can use a wok/deep pan).

Add cumin to the oil and as it turns brown, add this paste and gently fry the same.

As the paste starts giving off a nice aroma, add all the vegetables (cabbage, carrot, peas and potatoes) and sauté gently.

Add all the dry masala and salt to this mixture and keep stirring till all the vegetables are well coated.

Add the Ketchup and ghee to the mixture and stir again.

Add the water.

Close the lid with weight and bring it to full pressure on high.

Thereafter turn off the heat source.

(In case using a wok/deep pan, cover the wok/deep pan with a lid and reduce the heat to minimum. Let the vegetables cook to your liking for about 10 minutes. It is advised that you poke the vegetables once in a while with a fork to see whether they have been cooked.)

Let the cooker cool down on its own before opening it.

Your *band, gobi, gaajar, aloo mattar sabzi (cabbage, carrot, peas and potatoes veggie curry)* is ready.

Prep time: 10 minutes

Cooking time: 7 minutes with pressure cooker; 15-20 minutes with a wok/deep pan

Total time: 17 minutes with pressure cooker; 25-30 minutes with a wok/deep pan

Beans with coconut

This is a simple South Indian dish.

Ingredients

French beans-400 grams (14oz)

Grated fresh coconut-1

Chopped up Ginger-2 inches

Black Mustard Whole-1/2 teaspoon

Curry leaves-10

Cooking Oil-1 tablespoon

Salt to taste

Method

Wash the French beans thoroughly and cut them into one inch pieces. Steam the beans (for example, in a microwave steamer) for 5 minutes.

In a pan, add the cooking oil and put it on your heat source.

As soon as the oil warms up, add the mustard and curry leaves.

As the mustard splutters, add the ginger.

Stir for a minute.

Add the French beans, salt and the grated fresh coconut.

Mix and stir well. Your veggie is ready.

Prep time: 5 minutes

Cooking time: 8 minutes

Total time: 13 minutes

Cabbage, carrot and peas with coconut

Another tribute to South India.

Ingredients

Cabbage-400 grams (14oz)

Carrot-100 grams (3.5oz)

Peas shelled-100 grams (3.5oz)

Grated fresh coconut-1

Chopped up Ginger-2 inches

Black Mustard Whole-1/2 teaspoon

Curry leaves-10

Cooking Oil-1 tablespoon

Salt to taste

Method

Wash the Cabbage and Carrot thoroughly and cut them into one inch pieces.

Steam the cabbage, carrot and peas (for example, in a microwave steamer) for 5 minutes.

In a pan, add the cooking oil and put it on your heat source.

As soon as the oil warms up, add the mustard and curry leaves.

As the mustard splutters, add the ginger.

Stir for a minute.

Add the steamed vegetables, salt and the grated fresh coconut.

Mix and stir well.

Your veggie is ready.

Prep time: 5 minutes

Cooking time: 10 minutes

Total time: 15 minutes

Grilled Paneer (Cottage Cheese)

This JIFFY dish is for my Western friends, for introducing the taste of *Paneer* to them in a very familiar sauce.

Ingredients

Cottage cheese-200 grams (7oz)

Pizza/pasta sauce-1 tablespoon per piece

Salt to taste

Method

Slice the cottage cheese in such a way that they resemble half a slice of bread.

On each piece, sprinkle a little salt and cover it with a tablespoon of pizza/pasta sauce.

Marinate for 15 minutes.

Place the marinated pieces in a grill and grill for about 5 minutes or till the cottage cheese becomes slightly cooked.

That's all. Enjoy.

Prep time: 20 minutes for marinating and collecting all the ingredients together

Cooking time: 5 minutes

Total time: 25 minutes

Mattar Paneer (Cottage Cheese with peas in a curry)

This is the classic North Indian dish that you will find everywhere, in homes, *dhabas* as well as fancy restaurants. Here is a low calorie version, however.

Ingredients

Paneer (Cottage cheese)--1/2 Kg (500 grams or 18oz)

Green peas (shelled, fresh are preferred) --200 grams (7oz)

Medium size Onions--2

Garlic-4 pieces

Ginger-1 inch

Fresh tomato-2 (washed and chopped)

Turmeric (*Haldi*) - 1/2 tea spoon

Dry crushed coriander-2 tea spoon

Garam Masala (mixture of common Indian spices) crushed- 1/2   tea spoon

Kashmiri Red Chilli powder--1/4 tea spoon (Recommended for colour, but if you like your dish to be really spicy, use some other red chilli powder)

Cumin whole-1/2 tea spoon

Salt-1 level tea spoon (or to taste)

Tomato Ketchup-1 table spoon

Cooking oil-1 table spoon

Ghee (clarified butter)-1 tea spoon

Water-1 tea cup

Method

Take the *Paneer* (cottage cheese) and dry roast it in a non- stick pan till it turns a golden brown. It can then be cut into bite size pieces.

(Most recipes would advise that you fry these pieces in oil, which you can try if you don't mind the additional calories).

Blend together (in a blender preferably!) the onions, garlic, ginger and tomatoes to a fine paste.

Heat the oil in a pressure cooker. (In case you don't have a pressure cooker, you can use a wok or a deep pan).

Add cumin to the oil and as it turns brown, add this paste and gently fry the same.

As the paste starts giving off a nice aroma, add the peas and the cottage cheese and sauté gently.

Add all the dry masala and salt to this mixture.

Add the Ketchup and *Ghee* to the mixture and stir again.

Add the water, close the lid with weight and bring it to full pressure on high.

Turn off the heat.

Let the cooker cool down on its own before opening it.

(In case you are using a wok, add the water, cover the wok/pan with a lid and reduce the heat to minimum. Let the peas cook to your liking, which should take about 5 minutes).

Your *Mattar paneer* (cottage cheese with peas curry) is ready.

Prep time: 10 minutes

Cooking time: 5 minutes with pressure cooker, 10 minutes with a wok/pan

Total time: 15 minutes with pressure cooker, 20 minutes with a wok/pan

Mixed vegetables in coconut milk

If you want to be really adventurous, then try making this South Indian mixed vegetable curry in coconut milk. Believe me, it tastes so heavenly that it has become my personal favourite. And this 6-vegetable recipe with the goodness of coconut milk and so many Indian spices is healthy as well.

Ingredients

Pumpkin-150 grams (5oz)

Carrot-100 grams (3.5oz)

Beans-100 grams (3.5oz)

Cauliflower-100 grams (3.5oz)

Potato-100 grams (3.5oz)

Bottle Gourd-100 grams (3.5oz)

Onion-1

Ginger-1 inch

Garlic-4 cloves

Tomato-1

(Onion+ Ginger+ Garlic + tomato to be made into a fine paste in a blender)

Black Mustard seeds-1/2 teaspoon

Curry leaves-a few

Coriander powder-2 teaspoon

Turmeric powder-1 teaspoon

Red chilli powder-1/4 teaspoon

Coconut milk-400 ml (1 + ½ cups)

Cooking oil-2 tablespoon

Salt to taste

Method

Wash and cut the vegetables into bite size pieces.

Prepare your onion + garlic+ ginger + tomato paste.

Now place the pressure cooker/wok/deep pan on your heat source and add the cooking oil.

When the oil warms up, add the mustard seeds (*rai*) and the curry leaves.

When the *rai* splutters, add the onion + garlic+ ginger + tomato paste. Stir well.

Keep stirring till the paste is well fried and gives off a lovely aroma.

Add all the vegetables to this mixture and then again stir well.

Add the coriander, turmeric, red chilli powder and the salt.

Keep stirring till all the vegetables are well coated.

Now, add a little water and close the lid of the cooker.

Put the weight and let the cooker come to full pressure.

Switch off the heat source and release the pressure immediately, otherwise the veggies will be overcooked.

(In case of a wok/deep pan, add a little water, cover the wok/deep pan with a lid and reduce the heat to minimum. Let the vegetables cook to your liking for about 10 minutes. It is advised that you poke the vegetables once in a while with a fork to see that they have been cooked well.)

Open the cooker and now add the coconut milk.

Switch on the heat source and put the pressure cooker back on it once again (without covering it) till the vegetables come to a boil.

You can now finally switch off the heat source.

Your mixed vegetables in coconut milk is ready to be served.

(In case cooking in a wok or deep pan, you can add the coconut milk as soon as the

vegetables are cooked. Bring the mixture to a boil and your dish is ready).

Note: If you can manage to get some ready-made fried paste, you can certainly use that instead of frying the onion, garlic, ginger and tomato paste. In that case you simply add the paste to the mustard seeds (*rai*), add the vegetables to the mixture and then follow the rest of the instructions. This saves a lot of time as you don't have to brown the onion + garlic+ ginger + tomato paste.

Prep time: 10 minutes

Cooking time: 7 minutes with a pressure cooker, 15 minutes with wok/pan

Total time: 17 minutes with a pressure cooker, 25 minutes with wok/pan

Lauki Plain (Bottle Gourd)

This is the easiest way to cook *Lauki* the Eastern Indian way, with absolutely the minimum of spices. So no turmeric, no *garam masala* or *pachphoran*. Nothing can be simpler and still be so tasty.

Ingredients

Lauki (Bottle Gourd)--1 (roughly a kg or 2lb) cut into bite size pieces

Onion Medium—1 (chopped)

Jeera (Cumin)--1/2 teaspoon

Dry Red Whole (not powder) Chilli--1 (Just for flavour and not to make the food spicy)

Salt--1 level teaspoon (or to taste)

Cooking oil--1 tablespoon

Method

In a pressure cooker/**wok/deep pan**, add the cooking oil and when it warms up, add the cumin seeds (*jeera*) and the dry red whole chilli.

As soon as the cumin (*jeera*) starts browning, add the chopped onion and sauté it till it becomes translucent.

Add the *lauki* (gourd) pieces, and the salt. Stir well.

Close the pressure cooker's lid with weight and let it come to full pressure.

Immediately remove the pressure cooker from your heat source, cool it under running cold water and release the pressure.

Now open the lid and put the cooker back on fire. This is because the bottle gourd (*lauki*) gives out a lot of water. So let it dry up somewhat before you serve.

That's all.

(In case you are using a wok/deep pan, cover the wok/deep pan with a lid and reduce the heat to minimum. Since gourd leaves a lot of water, you don't need to add any additional water like you do with other vegetables. Let the gourd cook to your liking for about 10 minutes. It is advised that you poke it once in a while with a fork to see whether the gourd has been cooked well.)

Prep time: 5 minutes

Cooking time: 10 minutes with a pressure cooker; 15 minutes with a wok/pan

Total time: 15 minutes with a pressure cooker, 20 minutes with a wok/pan

Palak Baingan (Spinach-Aubergine)

This is a true blood Eastern India dish using *pachphoran*. You master this and you can then cook any other *pachphoran* recipe with élan.

Ingredients

Spinach (*Palak*)--1 Kg or 2lb (washed and chopped)

Aubergines (*Baingan*)-1 (roughly 200 grams or 7oz) (washed and cut into 1" cubes)

Onion Medium—1 (chopped)

Tomatoes--2 (washed and chopped)

Pachphoran, which is a mixture of *Jeera* (cumin), *Saunf* (fennel seeds), *Methi* seeds (fenugreek seeds), *Rai* (black mustard seeds), and *Kalonji* (onion seeds) in equal proportion--1 teaspoon

Cooking oil (preferably Mustard)--1 tablespoon full

Salt-1/2 teaspoon (or to taste)

Method

Heat oil in a pressure cooker/**wok/deep pan** and add the *Pachphoran*.

As the *Pachphoran* begins to splutter (which takes a few seconds), add the chopped onions and sauté on low flame for a minute.

Add the washed and chopped spinach, aubergine and the tomatoes.

Stir the same to evenly mix it.

Close the lid of the cooker with the weight and let it come to full pressure.

Immediately remove the pressure cooker from your heat source, cool it under running cold water and release the pressure.

Now open the lid and put the cooker back on fire. This is because Spinach gives out a lot of water. So let it dry up somewhat before you serve.

At this juncture add the salt and mix well. That's all.

(In case you are using a wok/deep pan, cover the wok/deep pan with a lid and reduce the heat to minimum. Since Spinach leaves a lot of water, you don't need to add any additional water like you do with other vegetables. Let the vegetables cook to your liking for about 10 minutes. At this juncture add the salt and mix well.)

Prep time: 5 minutes

Cooking time: 10 minutes with a pressure cooker, 15 minutes with a wok/deep pan

Total time: 15 minutes with a pressure cooker, 20 minutes with a wok/deep pan

Palak Paneer (Cottage Cheese in pureed spinach curry)

Another very popular North Indian dish that can be made as mild as you like it to be. This recipe is ideal for introducing the benefits of the humble Spinach to young people in your family, and that too in a really delicious manner.

Ingredients

Paneer (Cottage cheese)--1/2 Kg (500 grams or 18oz)

Spinach --1 Kg (2lb)

Medium size Onions—1 (chopped)

Garlic-4 pieces

Fresh tomato-1 (washed and chopped)

Garam Masala (mixture of common Indian spices) crushed- 1/2 tea spoon

Kashmiri Red Chilli powder--1/4 tea spoon (Recommended for colour, but if you like your dish to be really spicy, use some other red chilli powder)

Cumin seeds (*Jeera*)-1/2 tea spoon

Salt- to taste

Ghee (clarified butter)-2 tablespoon

Method

Take the *Paneer* (cottage cheese) and dry roast it in a non- stick pan till it turns a golden brown. It can then be cut into bite size pieces.

In a pressure cooker/wok/deep pan, put together the washed spinach, onions, garlic and tomatoes.

Please note that there is no need to add any water as spinach leaves a lot of water.

Put it on your heat source and bring to full pressure, that is, when the weight lifts and there is a whistling sound.

Remove the pressure cooker from your heat source, cool it under running cold water and release the pressure.

(In case using a wok/deep pan, cover the wok/deep pan with a lid. The moment you see the juices start to boil, reduce the heat to minimum and let the spinach cook for approximately 10 minutes in its own juice.

Pour all the cooked ingredients from the pressure cooker/**wok/deep pan** into a blender and blend well.

Place a clean wok (and not the one used for boiling the ingredients, unless you clean that first) on your heat source.

Add the clarified butter (*Ghee*).

As the clarified butter warms up, add the cumin seeds (*jeera*).

When the *Jeera* starts to brown, add the blended spinach mixture.

Thereafter add the *garam masala*, the red chilli powder and the salt. Mix well.

Add the roasted cottage cheese and let the curry come to a boil.

Switch off the heat source.

Your *Palak Paneer* is ready.

Relish this with rice or *rotis*.

Prep time: 5 minutes

Cooking time: 20 minutes with pressure cooker, 30 minutes with wok/deep pan

Total time: 25 minutes with pressure cooker, 35 minutes with wok/deep pan

Sarson Ka Saag (Mustard leaves dish)

This is another classic North Indian dish that goes well with *Makki di Roti* (Corn flour bread) or *Missi Roti* (Chick pea flour bread). Try this recipe if you want to put some zing to the humble spinach.

Ingredients

Mustard leaves (*Sarson ka saag*)-1 Kg (2lb)

Spinach-300 grams or 10oz (This is required to reduce the bitter taste of the mustard leaves.)

Chopped Onions-2

Garlic-4 cloves

Chopped Tomatoes-3

Turmeric (*Haldi*)-1/2 teaspoon

Red Chilli powder-1/2 teaspoon

Cumin seeds (*Jeera*)-1/2 teaspoon

Mustard Oil (preferred for the authentic taste)-1 tablespoon

Clarified Butter (*Ghee*)-1 tablespoon

Salt to taste

Water-1/2 cup

Method

Wash and chop the mustard leaves, spinach, 1 onion (of two), the garlic cloves and 2 tomatoes (out of 3).

Place these in a pressure cooker/**wok/deep pan** with ½ cup water.

Switch on the heat source and bring the pressure cooker to full pressure with the lid closed.

(In case, you don't have a pressure cooker, you can boil the above in a wok/deep pan with cover. The moment the water starts boiling, reduce the heat to minimum and let the spinach combo cook for approximately 5 more minutes in its own juice).

Switch off the heat.

When the ingredients in the cooker/**wok/deep pan** cool down, remove them and blend well in a blender.

Place a clean wok (and not the one used for boiling the ingredients, unless you clean that first) on fire.

Add the Mustard oil and clarified butter (*Ghee*).

When this warms up, add the cumin seeds (*Jeera*).

As soon as the seeds brown, add the left over chopped onions and fry well till the onions acquire a nice golden colour.

Add the left over tomato, the chilli powder and turmeric (*Haldi*).

Sauté well till the tomatoes soften up.

Add the blended ingredients and the salt (to taste).

Let the mixture come to a boil.

Switch off the heat source.

Your Mustard Spinach leaves dish (*Sarson Ka Saag*) is ready.

It tastes really good with most Indian breads, especially *Missi* (chick pea flour) roti.

Prep time: 10 minutes

Cooking time: 15 minutes with pressure cooker; 20 minutes with a wok/deep pan

Total time: 25 minutes with pressure cooker; 35 minutes with a wok/deep pan

Mashed Potato Southern Indian style

This recipe goes well as an accompaniment to various Southern Indian rice dishes.

Ingredients

Potatoes-1/2 kg (18oz)

Sliced Onion-1

Turmeric powder-1/2 teaspoon

Black Mustard-1/2 teaspoon

Curry leaves-a few

Tamarind paste-1 tablespoon dissolved in 1/2 cup water

Cooking Oil-1 tablespoon

Salt to taste

Whole Green chillies (just for flavour and not to make it hot)-1

Grated fresh coconut-3 tablespoon

Method

Boil and peel the potatoes and then mash it with a fork.

In a wok, put the cooking oil and put it on your heat source.

As soon as the oil warms up, add the mustard, the onions and the whole green chilli.

Sauté till the onion becomes translucent.

Then add the turmeric, the curry leaves, the grated coconut and the salt.

Sauté for a few more minutes.

Now, add the mashed potatoes and mix well.

Add the tamarind paste. This will impart a certain tartness to the potatoes and also help in mixing up all the ingredients together.

Let the mixture dry which should hardly take a minute or two.

Now, turn off the heat source and take out the mashed potatoes in a serving bowl.

Your mashed potato is ready.

Prep time: 5 minutes

Cooking time: 5 minutes (if potatoes are already boiled) otherwise include the time for boiling the potatoes.

Total time: 10 minutes

Aloo Gobi (Potato-Cauliflower)

This is a very popular North Indian dry veggie dish. Alone, it goes well with *Pooris* (fried non leavened Indian bread). Otherwise, it is paired with another curry dish and/or lentil dish and enjoyed with rice or *rotis*.

Ingredients

Potatoes-2

Cauliflower-1

Onion-1

Garlic-2

Ginger-1/2 inch

Turmeric (*Haldi*)-1/2 tea spoon

Garam Masala (mixture of common Indian spices) crushed- 1/2 teaspoon

Tomato-1

Salt-1/2 tea spoon (or to taste)

Cooking Oil-1 table spoon

Method

Cut the potatoes into small pieces and also separate the florets of the cauliflower.

Steam this for 5 minutes (in a microwave, use a microwave safe steamer for this).

Meanwhile, chop the onion, garlic, ginger and tomatoes.

In a wok, heat the oil, and add the chopped onion, garlic and ginger.

When this mixture starts becoming translucent, add the tomatoes and let the tomatoes cook.

Add the steamed vegetables to this and sprinkle *haldi, garam masala* and salt.

Let this all cook together for about 3 minutes.

A table spoon or two of water helps in blending all together.

That's all. Your dry *aloo gobi* is ready.

Note: Please note that if you don't steam the veggies first, you can proceed as above but you will then need triple the quantity of oil and will need to cook the vegetables for at least 15 minutes.

Prep time: 5 minutes

Cooking time: 15 minutes

Total time: 20 minutes

Aloo Bharta (Mashed Potato)

This typically Eastern India, or rather Bihari, dish is a must with *Khichdi*. I give a milder version here, but if you need to spice it up, then mix some stuffed red chilli pickles to this and enjoy.

Ingredients

Potatoes-1/2 kg (18oz)

Onion-1 (chopped finely)

Green chilli de-seeded (for flavour)-1 (Retain the seeds if you like it hot)

Fresh Coriander leaves-50 grams (2oz)

Mustard oil (if you want the authentic flavour)-1/2 teaspoon

Salt-to taste

Method

Boil and peel the potatoes, then mash it well.

Add the salt and the mustard oil.

Add the onion, chilies and coriander (all raw).

Mix well.

That's all. Your Bihari *Aloo Bharta* is ready.

Prep time: Only the time taken to boil and peel the potatoes and chop onions, etc.

Cooking time: No cooking time

Total time: 15 minutes maximum

Baigun Bhaja (Aubergine fries)

This too is a great accompaniment of the Eastern Indian *Khichdi*.

Ingredients

Fat round purple Aubergine-1

Turmeric-1 teaspoon

Salt- to taste

Rice flour-1 tablespoon full

Mustard Oil -3 tablespoon

Method

Finely slice the aubergine into round pieces.

Sprinkle the salt and turmeric on both sides.

Sprinkle the rice flour and again let it cover all pieces on all sides well.

In a non-stick frying pan, heat the oil and add the aubergine pieces.

Let it brown on one side and then turn it over and brown the other side equally well.

(If you need to handle more aubergines, then fry them batch wise.)

Gently remove from the pan and put it in a dish lined with an absorbent paper napkin. This helps in soaking up the excess oil from the aubergine.

Put these in a serving dish and enjoy your *baigun bhaja*.

Prep time: 5 minutes

Cooking time: 2 minutes@ each batch of aubergines to be fried

Total time: Approximately 12-15 minutes

Kohra (Plain Pumpkin Delight)

This Eastern Indian veggie is sweet, both literally and figuratively. Try this with *Pooris or Parathas* and I'm sure you will agree with me that ripe pumpkin made any other way can't taste so delicious.

Ingredients

Ripe yellow pumpkin-1 Kg (2lb)

Fenugreek seeds (*Methi*)-1/2 teaspoon

Coriander powder- 2 heap teaspoon

Turmeric powder-1 teaspoon

Kashmiri red chilli powder-1/2 teaspoon

Mango Dry powder (*Amchoor*)-1/2 teaspoon

Asafoetida powder (*Hing*)-1 level teaspoon

Cooking Oil-2 tablespoon

Water-1 cup

Sugar-3 teaspoon

Salt-1 teaspoon (or to taste)

Method

Peel the pumpkin and cut the flesh into bite size pieces.

Place a pressure cooker/**wok/deep pan** on the heat source and add the cooking oil.

When the cooking oil warms up, add the Fenugreek seeds (Methi) and thereafter add the pumpkins.

REMEMBER FENUGREEK SEEDS (METHI) BURN VERY FAST, SO DON'T LEAVE IT IN THE OIL WITHOUT THE PUMPKIN FOR MORE THAN A FEW SECONDS.

Now, add all the other ingredients and stir well for approximately 2 minutes to ensure that all the ingredients are well blended and very lightly fried.

Pour the water over the pumpkin and close the lid with weight.

Let the cooker come to full pressure.

Reduce the heat and let the cooker remain on minimum heat for 5 minutes.

Thereafter turn off the heat source and let the cooker cool on its own.

Open the lid and place the cooker back on the heat source without the lid.

Dry the pumpkin, that is, let the water evaporate till you have a nice thick consistency.

(In case you are using a wok/deep pan, pour the water, cover the wok/deep pan with a lid and reduce the heat to minimum. Let the

pumpkin cook to your liking for about 15 minutes. Dry the pumpkin, that is, let the water evaporate till you have a nice thick consistency.)

The delicious pumpkin dish is ready.

Prep time: 8 minutes

Cooking time: 15 minutes with a pressure cooker; 30 minutes with a wok/deep pan

Total time: 23 minutes with a pressure cooker; 38 minutes with a wok/deep pan

CHAPTER 8

FISH & FOWL

Anyone interacting with the peripatetic Indian businessmen, who hail predominantly from the western Indian states of Gujarat or Rajasthan, thinks Indians to be primarily vegetarians. Once in India, they are then justifiably shocked to find a flourishing omnivorous tradition.

Some attribute this to the influence of rulers who came from Turkey, Persia or any of the Central Asian States like Uzbekistan. This is evident from the very popular body of dishes that goes around under the banner of *Mughlai* cuisine.

Certainly much of the baking tradition, especially using *tandoors* (earthen ovens) would have come from these regions. But barbeque, I'm not so sure that it is not as ancient as the discovery of fire and roasting of the hunt-of-the-day thereon.

And what would you say to the South Indian and in fact the entire Coastal Indian tradition of cooking their meats and fishes with coconut, curry leaves and *Rai* (black mustard seeds)? And the Eastern Indian tradition of using *Pachphoran*? Original and quite unparalleled? Yes absolutely, because no West Asian or East Asian nation cooks like the South, West and East Indians do.

That leaves the North Indian cuisine which prima facie looks "influenced". I've, however, scoured the lanes of Samarkand and Bukhara for any *Mughlai* dish and failed. I couldn't even get a simple curry anywhere. There was no trace of *Dal Bukhara* (or any lentil dish) even in the priciest of restaurants in Bukhara. Yes, I could have *Rice Pilaf*, but they were sweet and made in cotton seed oil. These tasted so different from any Indian *Pulao or Biryani* that I am not sure whether the Central Asians inspired us or whether we taught them a trick or two. The kebabs contained NO spices. The desserts didn't use milk or milk products. I could go on and on...

Made me wonder if we are being too self-deprecatory and too generous in giving credit to "foreign" influences?

Before I spark off a major controversy, let me stop here and focus on the "Home Style" non-vegetarian dishes of my home.

Accordingly I present now six chicken, four fish, one mutton and one egg recipe spanning the Northern,

Eastern and Southern Indian traditions. You master this and you can handle any Indian non-vegetarian dish, I promise.

Basic Indian Chicken curry

This is the Basic North Indian Chicken Curry that once mastered can be easily adapted into a number of variations simply by adding or deleting some ingredients.

Ingredients

Whole chicken -1 (cut into 8 pieces)

Chopped Onion-3 large

Chopped Ginger-2 inch piece

Chopped Garlic-8 Cloves

Tomatoes-3

Coriander powder-2 teaspoon

Turmeric-1 teaspoon

Garam Masala-1 teaspoon

Tip: If you can't get ready-made *garam masala* mixture from a nearby Indian store, you can make yours by using 1 black cardamom, 3 green cardamoms, 4 cloves, and 1 inch cinnamon-all ground together for this dish.

Red chilli powder-1/4 teaspoon (enough only to add flavour and not to make it hot)

Cumin seeds-1/2 teaspoon

Tomato Ketchup-2 tablespoon

Cooking Oil-2 tablespoon

Ghee (Clarified butter)-1 tablespoon

Water-3 cups

Salt to taste

Method

In a pressure cooker, add the oil and the put it on your heat source.

As the oil turns hot, add the cumin seeds and let it splutter.

Immediately add the chopped onion.

Stir well till the onions become translucent.

Now, add the chopped ginger and garlic and stir till it starts giving off a nice aroma.

Add the chicken and the *ghee* (clarified butter).

 Stir well.

Add the coriander powder, turmeric, *garam masala* and red chilli powder.

Stir and cook the chicken till all the water evaporates and the chicken becomes almost dry. This process ensures that all the raw flavours of chicken, onions, etc. are removed.

Add now the tomatoes and the ketchup.

Stir well again and add the salt.

Let the tomatoes cook well.

Now, add the water, and close the lid of the pressure cooker with weight.

Let it come to full pressure (*i.e. when the weight lifts and there is a whistling sound*).

Immediately reduce the heat (to SIM on a gas stove) and let the chicken cook for 5 more minutes before turning off the heat source.

Let the cooker cool down on its own.

Note: If you don't have a pressure cooker, you can use a wok. Every step remains the same except for the last stage where cooking the chicken may take about 25-30 minutes (instead of 5 minutes in a pressure cooker) or till the chicken becomes tender.

Your basic chicken curry is now ready.

Prep time: 7 minutes

Cooking time: 10 minutes with pressure cooker; 25-30 minutes with wok

Total time: 17 minutes with pressure cooker; 32-37 minutes with wok

Thick Chicken curry

Ingredients

Whole chicken -1 approx. 800 grams or 28oz (cut into 8 pieces)

Onion-3 large (chopped)

Ginger-2 inch piece

Garlic-8 Cloves

Tomatoes-3 (chopped)

(Onion + Ginger + Garlic + Tomatoes blended and made into a fine paste)

Coriander powder-2 teaspoon

Turmeric-1 teaspoon

Garam Masala-1 teaspoon

Tip: If you can't get ready-made *garam masala* mixture from a nearby Indian store, you can make yours by using 1 black cardamom, 3 green cardamoms, 4 cloves, and 1 inch cinnamon-all ground together for this dish.

Red chilli powder-1/4 teaspoon (enough only to add flavour and not to make it spicy)

Cumin seeds-1/2 teaspoon

Potatoes-2 (skinned and cut into big pieces)

Cooking Oil-3 tablespoon

Ghee (Clarified butter)-1 tablespoon

Water-3 cups

Egg-1

Sugar-1/2 teaspoon

Salt to taste

Method

In a pressure cooker, add the oil and the put it on your heat source.

As the oil turns hot, add the cumin seeds and let it splutter.

Immediately add the Onion + Ginger + Garlic + Tomatoes fine paste.

Stir well till the paste starts giving off a nice aroma and you can see the oil ooze out from the sides.

Add the chicken and stir well.

Add the coriander powder, turmeric, *garam masala* and red chilli powder.

Cook the chicken till all the water evaporates and the chicken is dry.

Add the potatoes.

Stir well again and add the salt and the sugar.

Now, add the water.

Close the lid of the pressure cooker with weight and let it come to full pressure (*i.e. when the weight lifts and there is a whistling sound*).

Immediately reduce the heat (to SIM on a gas stove) and let the chicken cook for 5 more minutes before turning off the heat source.

Let the cooker cool down on its own.

Open the cooker and put it back on the flame.

Meanwhile, beat up the egg in a bowl.

As the curry comes to a boil, gently add the egg stirring continuously. Remove the dish from fire.

Note: If you don't have a pressure cooker, you can use a wok. Every step remains the same except for the last stage where cooking the chicken may take about 30-35 minutes (instead of 5 minutes in a pressure cooker) or till the chicken becomes tender.

Prep time: 10 minutes

Cooking time: 15 minutes with pressure cooker; 30-35 minutes in a wok

Total time: 25 minutes with pressure cooker; 40-45 minutes in a wok

Lava Chicken

This is our JIFFY version of the popular Butter Chicken or the British Chicken Tikka Masala, except that we don't use any tandoor, *garam masala*, and also no tear-jerking onions. The bright red curry will make this dish an instant hit with the young persons in your family.

Ingredients

Whole chicken -1 approx. 800 grams or 28oz (cut into 8 pieces)

Yoghurt-3 tablespoon

Chopped Ginger-1 inch piece

Chopped Garlic-6 cloves

Coriander powder-1 teaspoon

Red chilli powder-1/4 teaspoon (enough only to add flavour and not to make it spicy)

Cumin powder-1/2 teaspoon

Salt to taste

For the gravy:

Chopped Tomatoes-3 large ripe

Tomato puree-200 grams (7oz)

Low fat fresh cream-200 grams (7oz)

Butter-1 tablespoon

Coriander powder-1 teaspoon

Cumin powder-1/2 teaspoon

Red chilli powder-1/4 teaspoon (enough only to add flavour and not to make it spicy)

Salt and sugar to taste

Cashew nuts-50 grams or 2oz (fried golden and then chopped up. The method to fry the cashew nuts: in a small pan, add about a tablespoon of cooking oil. Put the pan on your heat source. When the oil heats up, add the cashew nuts and stir till they turn golden. Immediately remove the cashew nuts to a plate and chop. Remember if you leave the cashew nuts in the pan, the hot oil will keep roasting the cashew nuts and burn them.)

Method

Get the chicken ready

The first step to create this delectable dish is to make the chicken.

In a pressure cooker, put the chicken pieces with all the ingredients (EXCEPT FOR THE INGREDIENTS FOR THE GRAVY).

Mix well.

Note: You can also marinate the chicken for about 2 hours in the fridge with all these ingredients as that will help the chicken become tender. However, if you are short of time, you can also cook it instantly.

Close the lid of the pressure cooker with weight and put it on your heat source.

Let the cooker come to full pressure (i.e. when the weight lifts and there is a whistling sound).

Immediately reduce the heat (to SIM on a gas stove) and let the chicken cook for 5 more minutes before turning off the heat source.

Let the cooker cool down on its own.

If you are not using a pressure cooker, then you can use a wok but the chicken will take longer to cook (may be 20-25 minutes).

How to make the gravy

Meanwhile, take a wok and put it on your heat source.

Add the butter.

When the butter melts, add the coriander, cumin and the chilli powder.

Let the mixture roast for 1 minute.

Add the tomatoes and cook till the tomatoes soften up.

Add the tomato puree and the salt and sugar.

Gently keep stirring.

As the gravy turns a nice thick red colour, add the fresh low fat cream.

Stir well.

Switch off the heat source.

In a microwavable dish, mix together the cooked chicken and the gravy together.

Remember to add all the curry which may be there in the cooker as well.

Add the cashew nuts.

Microwave for 5 minutes so that all the ingredients are well integrated.

Your delicious chicken in a lava red curry with cashew nuts is ready.

Prep time: 7 minutes

Cooking time: 15 minutes with pressure cooker; 30-35 minutes in a wok; plus 5 minutes in the microwave for finishing

Total time: 27 minutes with pressure cooker; 42-47 minutes in a wok

Chicken in a Coconut curry

This is a South Indian style, chicken recipe. If you have had only North Indian style chicken so far, try this finger-licking good recipe with such exotic flavours that they will wow you over.

Ingredients

Whole chicken -1 approx. 800 grams or 28oz (cut into 8 pieces)

Onion-1 large (chopped)

Ginger-1 inch piece

Garlic-6 Cloves

Tomatoes-2 (chopped)

(Onion + Ginger + Garlic + Tomatoes blended and made into a fine paste)

Coriander powder-2 teaspoon

Turmeric-1 teaspoon

Garam Masala-1 teaspoon

Tip: If you can't get ready-made *garam masala* mixture from a nearby Indian store, you can make yours by using 1 black cardamom, 3 green cardamoms, 4 cloves, and 1 inch cinnamon-all ground together for this dish.

Red chilli powder-1/4 teaspoon (enough only to add flavour and not to make it spicy)

Black Mustard seeds-1/2 teaspoon

Curry leaves- 10-12

Coconut Milk-400 ml (1 + ½ cups)

Potatoes-2 (skinned and cut into small pieces)

Cooking Oil-3 tablespoon

Salt to taste

Method

In a pressure cooker, add the oil and the put it on your heat source.

As the oil turns hot, add the black mustard seeds and let it splutter.

Immediately add the Onion + Ginger + Garlic + Tomatoes fine paste.

Add the curry leaves and stir well till the paste starts giving off a nice aroma and you can see the oil ooze out from the sides.

Add the chicken and stir well.

Add the coriander powder, turmeric, *garam masala* and red chilli powder.

Cook the chicken till all the water evaporates and the chicken is dry.

Add the potatoes. Stir well again.

Now add the coconut milk and salt.

Close the lid of the pressure cooker with weight and let it come to full pressure (i.e. when the weight lifts and there is a whistling sound).

Immediately reduce the heat (to SIM on a gas stove) and let the chicken cook for 5 more minutes before turning off the heat source.

Let the cooker cool down on its own.

Note: If you don't have a pressure cooker, you can use a wok. Every step remains the same except for the last stage where cooking the chicken may take about 30-35 minutes (instead of 5 minutes in a pressure cooker) or till the chicken becomes tender.

Your chicken in coconut milk is ready.

Prep time: 10 minutes

Cooking time: 15 minutes with pressure cooker; 30-35 minutes in a wok

Total time: 25 minutes with pressure cooker; 40-45 minutes in a wok

Keema Mattar (Mince-Peas Curry)

Ingredients

Chicken/Mutton mince--1/2 Kg (500 grams or 18oz)

Green peas (shelled fresh are preferred) --200 grams (7oz)

Medium size Onions--2 (chopped)

Garlic-4 pieces

Ginger-1 inch

Fresh tomato-2 (chopped)

Turmeric (*Haldi*) - 1/2 tea spoon

Dry crushed coriander-2 tea spoon

Garam Masala (mixture of common Indian spices) crushed- 1/2   tea spoon

Tip: If you can't get ready-made *garam masala* mixture from a nearby Indian store, you can make yours by using 1 black cardamom, 3 green cardamoms, 4 cloves, and 1 inch cinnamon-all ground together for this dish.

Kashmiri Red Chilli powder--1/4 tea spoon (Recommended for colour, but if you like your dish to be really spicy, use any other red chilli powder)

Curd (Indian style yoghurt)-1 table spoon

Cumin whole *(Jeera)*-1/2 tea spoon

Salt-1 level tea spoon (or to taste)

Tomato Ketchup-1 table spoon

Cooking oil-1 table spoon

Ghee (clarified butter)-1 tea spoon

Water-1 tea cup

Method

Blend together (in a blender preferably!) the onions, garlic, ginger and tomatoes to a fine paste.

Heat the oil in a pressure cooker/**wok/deep pan**.

Add cumin to the oil and as it turns brown, add this paste and gently fry the same.

As the paste starts giving off a nice aroma, add the mince to it and sauté gently.

Add all the dry *garam masala*, salt and curd to this mixture and keep stirring on low flame (SIM on a gas stove) till it starts becoming dry.

Add the Ketchup and peas to the mixture and stir again.

At this juncture, add the *Ghee* for a lovely taste.

Add the water, close the lid with *weight* (in case using a pressure cooker) and bring it to full pressure on high flame.

Thereafter cook on low flame (SIM on a gas stove) for 3 minutes, if it is chicken mince. And if it is mutton mince, cook it for a full 5 minutes. Let the cooker cool down on its own before opening it.

In case you are using a wok/deep pan, cover that with a tight fitting lid and cook for about 20 minutes or till the mince is completely cooked.

Prep time: 7 minutes

Cooking time: 10 minutes with pressure cooker; 20 minutes with a wok/deep pan

Total time: 17 minutes with pressure cooker; 27 minutes with a wok/deep pan

Chicken Kofta (Mince Ball) Curry

The chicken *kofta* curry is another variation of the famous Indian chicken curry. *Kofta* is basically a kind of a meatball (in this case a chicken meat ball) that is made with chicken mince, egg, *garam masala*, salt and bread slices.

Ingredients

Chicken mince -1/2 Kg (18oz)

Onion-2 large (chopped)

Ginger-2 inch piece

Garlic-8 Cloves

Tomatoes-3 (chopped)

(Onion + Ginger + Garlic + Tomatoes blended and made into a fine paste)

Coriander powder-2 teaspoon

Turmeric-1 teaspoon

Garam Masala-1+1/2 teaspoon

Tip: If you can't get ready-made *garam masala* mixture from a nearby Indian store, you can make yours by using 2 black cardamom, 4 green cardamoms, 6 cloves, and 1.5 inch cinnamon-all ground together for this dish.

Red chilli powder-1/4 teaspoon (enough only to add flavour and not to make it spicy)

Cumin seeds-1/2 teaspoon

Cooking Oil-3 tablespoon

Ghee (Clarified butter)-1 tablespoon

Water-3 cups

Bread-2 slices soaked in water

Egg-1

Sugar-1/2 teaspoon

Salt to taste

Method

In a bowl, mix together the chicken mince, one egg, half teaspoon *garam masala* and salt.

Add the bread slices after squeezing out all the water.

Make into walnut size balls.

In a frying pan, add the cooking oil and gently fry these balls 2-3 at a time and keep it in a plate.

Switch off the heat source.

In a pressure cooker, pour the oil from the pan and put it on your heat source.

As the oil turns hot, add the cumin seeds and let it splutter.

Immediately add the Onion + Ginger + Garlic + Tomatoes fine paste.

Stir well till the paste starts giving off a nice aroma and you can see the oil ooze out from the sides.

Add the coriander powder, turmeric, remaining 1 spoon of *garam masala* and red chilli powder.

Stir well again and add the salt and the sugar.

Now, add the water.

As the mixture comes to a boil, gently add the fried chicken balls.

Close the lid of the pressure cooker with weight and let it come to full pressure (i.e. when the weight lifts and there is a whistling sound).

Immediately reduce the heat (to SIM on a gas stove) and let the chicken balls cook for 2 more minutes before turning off the heat source.

Let the cooker cool down on its own.

In case you are using a wok/deep pan, cover that with a tight fitting lid and cook for about 20 minutes or till the *Kofta* is completely cooked.

Prep time: 10 minutes

Cooking time: 10 minutes with pressure cooker; 20 minutes with a wok

Total time: 20 minutes with pressure cooker; 30 minutes with a wok

Roasted "*Tandoori*" Chicken

Roast chicken is a great favourite of the British and *Tandoori* chicken is a ubiquitous dish that all restaurants from 5-star to wayside eateries in India serve with equal felicity. This recipe tries to combine the deliciousness of the roast chicken with the tanginess of the *tandoori*, without requiring you to invest in a *Tandoor* (a big earthen oven).

Ingredients

Whole Chicken -1 but cut into 8 pieces (or choose your favourite pieces)

Yoghurt-200 grams (7oz)

Ginger-2 inches chopped finely

Garlic-6 cloves chopped finely

Tomato sauce/ketchup-2 tablespoon

Garam Masala-1/2 teaspoon

Tip: If you can't get ready-made *garam masala* mixture from a nearby Indian store, you can make yours by using 1 black cardamom, 3 green cardamoms, 4 cloves, and 1 inch cinnamon-all ground together for this dish.

Kashmiri Red chilli powder (not hot variety)-1/4 teaspoon

Salt to taste

Juice of Lemon-1

Ghee (clarified butter) or butter (or any oil)-1 tablespoon

Method

In a bowl, beat together all the ingredients EXCEPT the chicken.

In a pressure cooker, add the chicken and the beaten ingredients together (unlike traditional *tandoori* chicken, you don't need to marinate the chicken with the beaten ingredients first).

Close the lid of the pressure cooker with weight and put it on your heat source.

Let it come to full pressure (*i.e. when the weight lifts and there is a whistling sound*).

Immediately reduce the heat (to SIM on a gas stove) and let the chicken cook for 5 more minutes before turning off the heat source.

Let the cooker cool down on its own.

Note: If you don't have a pressure cooker, you can use a wok. Every step remains the same except for the last stage where cooking the chicken may take about 20-25 minutes (instead of 5 minutes in a pressure cooker) or till the chicken becomes tender.

In a big non-stick pan, add the butter and put it on your heat source.

Let the butter melt.

Slowly add the chicken and the juices from the cooker/**pan/wok**.

Let all the water evaporate.

Gently turn the chicken to give it a golden brown colour.

Your Roasted "*Tandoori*" Chicken is now ready.

Prep time: 10 minutes

Cooking time: 20 minutes with a pressure cooker; 40-45 minutes with a wok

Total time: 30 minutes with a pressure cooker; 50-55 minutes with a wok

Egg Potato Curry (Serves 3 or 4 persons)

Ingredients

Egg-6 Hard boiled

Potatoes-2 boiled and cut into pieces

Chopped Onion-1

Chopped Ginger-1 inch

Chopped Garlic-4 cloves

Chopped Tomatoes-3

Garam Masala-1/2 teaspoon

Tip: If you can't get ready-made *garam masala* mixture from a nearby Indian store, you can make yours by using 1 black cardamom, 3 green cardamoms, 4 cloves, and 1 inch cinnamon-all ground together for this dish.

Turmeric powder (*Haldi*)-1/2 teaspoon

Red Chilli powder -1/4 teaspoon (This quantity only adds some flavour but does not make the food hot. You may add more if you like.)

Tomato Ketchup-1 tablespoon

Cooking Oil-2 tablespoon

Water-1 cup

Salt to taste

Method

In a blender, blend together the chopped onion, ginger, garlic and tomatoes and make into a fine paste.

In a wok, add the cooking oil and put it on your heat source.

When the oil becomes hot, add the hard boiled eggs and fry gently.

Remove the eggs from oil and keep it in a plate.

Add the onion+ ginger + garlic +tomato paste to the same oil.

Fry well till you get a nice aroma from the paste.

Add the rest of the ingredients and stir well.

Now, add the eggs, boiled potatoes with a cup of water and salt to taste.

When this comes to a boil, turn off the heat source.

Your egg curry is ready.

Prep time: 10 minutes

Cooking time: 10 minutes

Total time: 20 minutes

Basic Fish Fry

This Eastern Indian Fish Fry recipe is the mildest of all such recipes. You could add yellow mustard seed paste, garlic paste and red chilli powder to spice it up further and turn this into the fiery *Bihari Machheriabhujan*. Roll it up in *besan* (chick pea flour) batter, and fry to have the *Amritsari* Fish Fry or Fish *Pakodas*.

The variations can be as mindboggling as there are regions in India!

Ingredients

Sliced Fish-1/2 Kg (18oz)

Turmeric (*Haldi*)-1 teaspoon

Kashmiri Red Chilli powder-1/2 teaspoon (This imparts more colour and flavour and does not make it hot).

Salt to taste

Mustard Oil (preferred, otherwise use any other oil that you like) - 3 tablespoon

Method

Sprinkle salt, turmeric and *Kashmiri Red Chilli* powder on the fish to coat it.

Note: If refrigerated, please bring the fish to room temperature first.

Heat 3 tablespoon of oil in a wok/deep non-stick pan and gently fry the fish @ only 2-3 pieces of fish at a time.

After the fish turns a nice golden brown, remove to a plate and add the next batch to the oil.

Please ensure that the fish does not burn.

Your simple fish fry is ready.

Prep time: 3 minutes

Cooking time: 2 minutes @ each batch

Total time: Approximately 10 minutes

Machher Jhol (Fish Cooked in a Light Curry)

A simple fish curry from Eastern India that is eaten almost daily in many homes in West Bengal. This recipe uses a little bit of *garam masala* but no *pachphoran*.

Ingredients

Sliced Fish --1/2 kg (18oz)

Tomatoes -2 (to be made into a paste)

Onion-1 small (chopped)

Garlic-2 pieces

Ginger-1 inch

(Onion+ Garlic + Ginger to be made into a paste in a blender)

Salt--1 teaspoon (or to taste)

Sugar--1/4 teaspoon

Coriander powder--1 teaspoon

Garam Masala- 1/2 teaspoon

Turmeric (*Haldi*)--1 and 1/2 teaspoon (1 teaspoon for marinating the fish and half for the curry).

Red Chilli powder-- 1/4 teaspoon

Fresh green chillies whole--4 (Whole chillies only impart a lovely flavour to the cuisine and will NOT make it spicy)

Mustard oil--3 tablespoon (If you want that classic taste, otherwise whatever oil you normally use)

Cumin seeds (*Jeera*)-1 teaspoon

Water-1 glass (roughly 300 ml)

Vessels: One non-stick frying pan and one *kadai* (wok)

Method

Sprinkle 1/2 teaspoon of salt and 1 teaspoon of the turmeric on the fish to coat it on all sides.

Heat 2 tablespoon of oil (the third tablespoon to be used for making the curry) in a non-stick pan and gently fry the fish @ only 2-3 pieces of fish at a time.

After the fish turns a nice golden brown, remove to a plate and add the next batch to the oil.

Please ensure that the fish does not burn.

In a wok, add the oil left from frying (make sure the oil is clean and there are no pieces of fish in it) as well as the fresh third table spoon of oil.

Put the wok on your heat source.

As the oil heats up, add the cumin seeds and let it brown.

Do please make sure it does not burn.

Add onion+ garlic + ginger paste and stir well.

Add the salt, turmeric powder, coriander powder, red chilli powder, *garam masala* and sugar.

Keep on stirring till the paste is fried and you can see the oil glistening on the sides of the wok.

Add the tomato paste and stir well till the tomato is cooked.

Add 1 glass of water.

Add the fried fish to this mixture and also add the whole fresh green chillies.

When the mixture comes to a boil, reduce the heat to the minimum (SIM on a gas stove) and cook it for 2 more minutes.

Your classic *Machher Jhol* is ready.

Prep time: 5 minutes

Cooking time: 10 minutes

Total time: 15 minutes

Tamater Sarson Machhali (Fish Cooked In a Tangy Tomato and Mustard Sauce)

This is another very popular recipe from the Eastern Indian state of West Bengal using *Pachphoran*.

Ingredients

Sliced Fish --1/2 kg (18oz)

Tomatoes-3 chopped up

Onion-1 (chopped)

Garlic-4 pieces (Tomatoes + Onion+ Garlic made into a paste in a blender)

Mustard paste--4 table spoon (*Kasundi*-ready-made paste is preferred; otherwise just use English mustard paste)

Salt--1 teaspoon (or to taste)

Sugar--1/4 teaspoon

Fresh green chillies whole--4 (Whole chillies only impart a lovely flavour to the cuisine and will NOT make it spicy)

Mustard oil (or your preferred cooking oil)--3 tablespoon

Turmeric (*Haldi*)--1 teaspoon

Pachphoran: mixture of five spices, that is, *jeera* (cumin seeds), *saunf* (fennel seeds), *methi* seeds (fenugreek seeds), *rai* (black mustard seeds), *kalonji* (onion seeds)--all mixed in equal proportion: 1 teaspoon

Water- 1 glass (roughly 300 ml)

Vessels: One non-stick frying pan and one *kadai* (wok)

Method

Sprinkle 1/2 teaspoon of salt and all the turmeric on the fish to coat it on all sides.

Heat 2 tablespoon of oil (the third tablespoon to be used for making the curry) in a non- stick pan and gently fry the fish @ only 2-3 pieces of fish at a time. After the fish turns a nice golden brown, remove to a plate and add the next batch to the oil.

Please ensure that the fish does not burn.

In a wok, add the oil left from frying (make sure the oil is clean and there are no pieces of fish in it) as well as the fresh third table spoon of oil.

Put the wok on your heat source.

As the oil heats up, add the *Pachphoran* and let it brown (which takes only a few seconds). Do please make sure it does not burn.

Add the tomatoes + onion+ garlic paste and stir well.

Add the salt and sugar.

Keep on stirring till the paste is fried and you can see the oil glistening on the sides of the wok.

Add the Mustard paste and stir well.

Add a glass of water.

Add the fried fish to this mixture.

Also add the whole fresh green chillies.

When the mixture comes to a boil, reduce the heat to the minimum (SIM on a gas stove) and cook it for 2 more minutes.

That's all. Your *Tamater Sarson* Fish is ready.

Prep time: 5 minutes

Cooking time: 10 minutes

Total time: 15 minutes

Dahi Sarson Machhali (Fish cooked in a Yoghurt and Mustard paste)

Our tribute to yet another timeless Fish preparation from West Bengal. This dish neither uses *garam masala* nor *pachphoran*.

Ingredients

Sliced Fish --1/2 kg (18oz)

Yoghurt--400 grams (14oz)

Mustard paste--4 table spoon (*Kasundi*-ready-made paste is preferred; or just use English mustard paste)

Milk--1/2 cup

Salt--1 and 1/2 teaspoon (or to taste)

Sugar--1 teaspoon

Fresh green chillies whole--4 (Whole chillies only impart a lovely flavour to the cuisine and will NOT make it spicy)

Mustard oil (or your preferred cooking oil)--3 tablespoon

Turmeric (*Haldi*)--1 teaspoon

Vessels: One non-stick frying pan and one *kadai* (wok)

Method

Sprinkle 1/2 teaspoon of salt and all the turmeric on the fish to coat it on all sides.

Heat 2 tablespoon of oil (the third tablespoon to be used as raw oil later on) in a non-stick pan and gently fry the fish @ only 2-3 pieces of fish at a time.

After the fish turns a nice golden brown, remove to a plate and add the next batch to the oil. Please ensure that the fish does not burn.

The remaining oil can be strained and kept in the fridge to be used for frying more fish within the next week or so. It can't be used for anything else because of the fishy smell.

In a wok, beat up the yoghurt, mustard paste, milk, salt and sugar to a smooth blend.

Add the raw mustard oil to this mixture. Add the fried fish to this mixture and also add the whole fresh green chillies.

When the mixture comes to a boil, reduce the heat to the minimum (sim on a gas stove) and cook it for 2 more minutes. That's all. Your *Dahi Sarson* Fish is ready.

Prep time: 5 minutes

Cooking time: 10 minutes

Total time: 15 minutes

Fish Kerala style

This is our tribute to the robust fish eating tradition of Kerala, the southernmost state of India.

Ingredients

Fish-1/2 Kg (18oz) cut into pieces

Chopped Onion-1

Chopped Ginger-2 inch

Coconut Milk-200 ml (1 cup approximately)

Coconut powder-2 tablespoon

Lemon juice-1

Mustard seeds-1/2 teaspoon

Curry leaves-few

Salt to taste

Cooking Oil -2 tablespoon (Use a milder flavoured oil such as groundnut, sesame, or coconut for the best effect)

Method

Sprinkle a little salt on the fish pieces.

In a wok, add 2 tablespoon full of cooking oil and gently fry the fish in batches.

The fish should only have a light golden colour.

After removing the fish to a separate plate, add the mustard seeds to the same wok using the same cooking oil, until they crackle.

Immediately add the chopped onion and ginger and stir well.

Sauté for a few minutes and add the curry leaves.

Add the coconut milk and the coconut powder (dissolve the powder in water beforehand).

Add the fish and the salt.

Let the mixture come to a boil.

Reduce heat and cook for 2 minutes.

Switch off the heat source.

Add the lemon juice and your fish is ready.

This dish goes really well with plain rice.

Prep time: 5 minutes

Cooking time: 10 minutes

Total time: 15 minutes

CHAPTER 9

SNACKS AND ACCOMPANIMENTS

I t's time now to take up the side dishes.

This in India doesn't mean rice or boiled corn, because as we mentioned, rice or *rotis* would occupy quite a pride of place on the main platter.

On the other hand, Indian accompaniments are those *chutneys* (sauces), *raitas* (yoghurt based dish), *papadams*, and pickles without which an Indian *thali* (platter) would be considered incomplete. You basically take a bite of these in between your main meal to wake up your taste buds and to cleanse your palate, so to say.

Then there are these Indian snacks like *Pakoras* (vegetable fritters) or *Chiura/Poha* (savoury rice flakes) that you get served when you visit someone's home in North India. In wayside eateries, you may also see some *Aloo* (potato) or *Paneer* (cottage cheese) *Tikkis* (cutlets) being sizzled on huge pans.

If you crave for any of these sinful snacks, sauces and accompaniments, then do read on for some really idiot proof recipes.

We present 17 gems: 7 types of *Pakoras*, 1 *Poha/Chiura* dish, 2 *Tikkis*, 3 *Chutneys*, and 4 kinds of *Raitas*.

Pakoras (Vegetable Fritters)

Vegetable Fritters are a very popular snack to be eaten along with a nice hot cup of tea especially on a cool rainy day. All kinds of vegetables can be used for this tasty snack. We present some seven of the most popular ones.

Onion Pakoras

Ingredients

Chick pea flour-1 cup

Rice flour-1/2 cup

Baking powder-1/2 teaspoon

Asafoetida (*Hing*)-1/2 teaspoon

Coriander powder-1 teaspoon

Cumin seeds (*Jeera*)-1/2 teaspoon

Turmeric (*Haldi*)-1/2 teaspoon

Red Chilli powder-1/2 teaspoon

Salt-1/2 teaspoon

Water-1 cup (approximately)

Sliced Onions-4

Oil for deep frying

Method

Mix all the ingredients well except the onions. Add the water and beat until smooth and light.

It should be of a thin coating consistency. Set it aside for at least 15 minutes. This helps the flour to absorb the water well and attain a thicker consistency.

If it becomes too thick, you may add a little more water and beat well. Add the onions to this batter.

Heat oil in a frying pan or wok.

Take the mixture with the onion slices, a tablespoonful at a time and drop into the hot oil.

Be careful of the splatter that follows. You will find that the fritters swell up.

Gently turn them around and take out from the oil when they are nice and golden brown.

Remove to a dish which is covered with a paper napkin so that all the excess oil can be absorbed. Repeat till all the fritters/*pakoras* are fried. Enjoy with any of the chutneys, specially the mint chutney.

Prep time: 20 minutes

Cooking time: 3 minutes @ each batch

Total time: Approximately 30 minutes

Paneer Pakoras (Cottage Cheese fritters)

Ingredients

Chick pea flour-1 cup

Rice flour-1/2 cup

Baking powder-1/2 teaspoon

Asafoetida (*Hing*)-1/2 teaspoon

Coriander powder-1 teaspoon

Cumin seeds (*Jeera*)-1/2 teaspoon

Turmeric (*Haldi*)-1/2 teaspoon

Red Chilli powder-1/2 teaspoon

Salt-1/2 teaspoon

Water-1 cup (approximately)

Paneer (Cottage Cheese)-300 grams (10oz)

Oil for deep frying

Method

Mix all the ingredients well except the *paneer*.

Add the water and beat until smooth and light.

It should be of a thin coating consistency. Set it aside for at least 15 minutes. This helps the flour to absorb the water well and attain a thicker consistency.

If it becomes too thick, you may add a little more water and beat well.

Slice the *paneer* into bite size pieces and add to the batter.

Heat oil in a frying pan or wok.

Take the mixture with the *paneer* a tablespoonful at a time and drop into the hot oil.

Be careful of the splatter that follows.

You will find that the fritters swell up.

Gently turn them around and take out from the oil when they are nice and golden brown.

Remove to a dish which is covered with a paper napkin so that all the excess oil can be absorbed.

Repeat till all the fritters/*pakoras* are fried.

Enjoy with any of the chutneys.

Prep time: 20 minutes

Cooking time: 3 minutes @ each batch

Total time: Approximately 30 minutes

Palak Pakoras (Spinach fritters)

Ingredients

Chick pea flour-1 cup

Rice flour-1/2 cup

Baking powder-1/2 teaspoon

Asafoetida (*Hing*)-1/2 teaspoon

Coriander powder-1 teaspoon

Cumin seeds (*Jeera*)-1/2 teaspoon

Turmeric (*Haldi*)-1/2 teaspoon

Red Chilli powder-1/2 teaspoon

Salt-1/2 teaspoon

Water-1 cup (approximately)

Spinach (only leaves)-300 grams (10oz)

Oil for deep frying

Method

Mix all the ingredients, except the spinach, well.

Add the water and beat until smooth and light.

It should be of a thin coating consistency. Set it aside for at least 15 minutes. This helps the flour to absorb the water well and attain a thicker consistency.

If it becomes too thick, you may add a little more water and beat well.

Add the spinach to this batter.

Heat oil in a frying pan or wok. Take the mixture with the spinach a leaf at a time and drop into the hot oil.

Be careful of the splatter that follows.

You will find that the fritters swell up.

Gently turn them around and take out from the oil when they are nice and golden brown.

Remove to a dish which is covered with a paper napkin so that all the excess oil can be absorbed.

Repeat till all the fritters/*pakoras* are fried.

Enjoy with any of the *chutneys*.

Prep time: 20 minutes

Cooking time: 3 minutes @ each batch

Total time: Approximately 30 minutes

Gobi Pakoras (Cauliflower Fritters)

Ingredients

Chick pea flour-1 cup

Rice flour-1/2 cup

Baking powder-1/2 teaspoon

Asafoetida (*Hing*)-1/2 teaspoon

Coriander powder-1 teaspoon

Cumin seeds (*Jeera*)-1/2 teaspoon

Turmeric (*Haldi*)-1/2 teaspoon

Red Chilli powder-1/2 teaspoon

Salt-1/2 teaspoon

Water-1 cup (approximately)

Cauliflower-1 (with florets separated into bite size)

Oil for deep frying

Method

Mix all the ingredients, except the cauliflower, well.

Add the water and beat until smooth and light.

It should be of a thin coating consistency. Set it aside for at least 15 minutes. This helps the flour to absorb the water well and attain a thicker consistency.

If it becomes too thick, you may add a little more water and beat well.

Add the cauliflower to this batter.

Heat oil in a frying pan or wok.

Take the mixture with the cauliflower a tablespoonful at a time and drop into the hot oil.

Be careful of the splatter that follows.

You will find that the fritters swell up.

Gently turn them around and take out from the oil when they are nice and golden brown.

Remove to a dish which is covered with a paper napkin so that all the excess oil can be absorbed.

Repeat till all the fritters/*pakoras* are fried.

Enjoy with any of the chutneys.

Prep time: 20 minutes

Cooking time: 3 minutes @ each batch

Total time: Approximately 30 minutes

Baingan Pakoras (Aubergine Fritters)

Ingredients

Chick pea flour-1 cup

Rice flour-1/2 cup

Baking powder-1/2 teaspoon

Asafoetida (*Hing*)-1/2 teaspoon

Coriander powder-1 teaspoon

Cumin seeds (*Jeera*)-1/2 teaspoon

Turmeric (*Haldi*)-1/2 teaspoon

Red Chilli powder-1/2 teaspoon

Salt-1/2 teaspoon

Water-1 cup (approximately)

Round big Aubergines-2 (thinly sliced)

Oil for deep frying

Method

Mix all the ingredients, except the aubergines, well.

Add the water and beat until smooth and light.

It should be of a thin coating consistency. Set it aside for at least 15 minutes. This helps the flour to absorb the water well and attain a thicker consistency.

If it becomes too thick, you may add a little more water and beat well.

Add the aubergines to this batter.

Heat oil in a frying pan or wok.

Take the mixture with the aubergine a piece at a time and drop into the hot oil.

Be careful of the splatter that follows.

You will find that the fritters swell up.

Gently turn them around and take out from the oil when they are nice and golden brown.

Remove to a dish which is covered with a paper napkin so that all the excess oil can be absorbed.

Repeat till all the fritters/*pakoras* are fried.

Enjoy with any of the chutneys.

Prep time: 20 minutes

Cooking time: 3 minutes @ each batch

Total time: Approximately 30 minutes

Aloo Pakoras (Potato Fritters)

Ingredients

Chick pea flour-1 cup

Rice flour-1/2 cup

Baking powder-1/2 teaspoon

Asafoetida (*Hing*)-1/2 teaspoon

Coriander powder-1 teaspoon

Cumin seeds (*Jeera*)-1/2 teaspoon

Turmeric (*Haldi*)-1/2 teaspoon

Red Chilli powder-1/2 teaspoon

Salt-1/2 teaspoon

Water-1 cup (approximately)

Potatoes-4 (thinly sliced)

Oil for deep frying

Method

Mix all the ingredients, except the potatoes, well.

Add the water and beat until smooth and light.

It should be of a thin coating consistency. Set it aside for at least 15 minutes. This helps the flour to absorb the water well and attain a thicker consistency.

If it becomes too thick, you may add a little more water and beat well.

Add the potatoes to this batter.

Heat oil in a frying pan or wok.

Take the mixture with the potatoes a piece at a time and drop into the hot oil.

Be careful of the splatter that follows.

You will find that the fritters swell up.

Gently turn them around and take out from the oil when they are nice and golden brown.

Remove to a dish which is covered with a paper napkin so that all the excess oil can be absorbed.

Repeat till all the fritters/*pakoras* are fried.

Enjoy with any of the chutneys.

Prep time: 20 minutes

Cooking time: 3 minutes @ each batch

Total time: Approximately 30 minutes

Lauki Pakoras (Bottle Gourd Fritters)

Ingredients

Chick pea flour-1 cup

Rice flour-1/2 cup

Baking powder-1/2 teaspoon

Asafoetida (*Hing*)-1/2 teaspoon

Coriander powder-1 teaspoon

Cumin seeds (*Jeera*)-1/2 teaspoon

Turmeric (*Haldi*)-1/2 teaspoon

Red Chilli powder-1/2 teaspoon

Salt-1/2 teaspoon

Water-1 cup (approximately)

Lauki (Bottle Gourd)-1 (thinly sliced)

Oil for deep frying

Method

Mix all the ingredients, except the bottle gourd, well.

Add the water and beat until smooth and light.

It should be of a thin coating consistency. Set it aside for at least 15 minutes. This helps the flour to absorb the water well and attain a thicker consistency.

If it becomes too thick, you may add a little more water and beat well.

Add the gourd to this batter.

Heat oil in a frying pan or wok.

Take the mixture with the gourd a piece at a time and drop into the hot oil.

Be careful of the splatter that follows.

You will find that the fritters swell up.

Gently turn them around and take out from the oil when they are nice and golden brown.

Remove to a dish which is covered with a paper napkin so that all the excess oil can be absorbed.

Repeat till all the fritters/*pakoras* are fried.

Enjoy with any of the chutneys.

Prep time: 20 minutes

Cooking time: 3 minutes @ each batch

Total time: Approximately 30 minutes

Chiura or Poha Fry (Savoury Rice Flakes)

This is a very popular snack of Maharashtra as well as of Bihar.

Ingredients

Rice Flakes (*Chiura/Poha*)-1 cup

Raw peanuts-1/2 cup

Salt and pepper to taste

Oil-1/2 cup

Method

In a wok or sauce pan, heat the oil and fry the peanuts till golden brown. Do not let the peanuts brown too much or the peanuts will start tasting bitter.

Please remember the peanuts keep cooking in their own heat even when the peanuts are out of the pan.

Now in the same oil, add the rice flakes about a tablespoon at a time. As soon as these puff up, remove to a plate covered with a paper napkin to absorb the excess oil.

Repeat till all the rice flakes are fried.

In a bowl, mix together the peanuts and the rice flakes. Add the salt and pepper while the flakes are still warm otherwise the salt will not stick well to the flakes.

Let this mixture cool down. You can now store it (up to a week) in air tight containers to be used whenever you feel like having a savoury snack.

In addition to peanuts, you can also add cashew nuts/almonds following the same methodology.

In place of any of these nuts, you can also add some fresh peas simply sautéed with butter and cumin seeds. But this will have to be eaten fresh as the peas will not store that well as the nuts mentioned above.

Prep time: 2 minutes

Cooking time: 2 minutes

Total time: 4 minutes

Aloo Tikki (Potato Cutlets Indian style)

Ingredients

Boiled potatoes-500 grams (18oz)

Bread pieces-2

Chopped Onion-1

Green chillies (chopped and de-seeded)-2

Cumin seeds (*Jeera*)-1/2 teaspoon

Chopped Fresh Coriander Leaves-A small bunch

Lemon juice-1 tablespoon

Salt to taste

Cooking Oil-2 tablespoon

Method

Mash the boiled potatoes well.

Soak the bread pieces in water. Squeeze the water from the bread with both hands and then add to the boiled potatoes.

Add all the other ingredients and mix well.

Shape the mashed potato mixture into small flat patties.

In a shallow non-stick pan, heat the cooking oil and place the patties.

Brown the patties evenly on both sides and remove to a dish covered with an absorbent paper napkin.

Repeat till all the patties are cooked.

Serve hot with *chutneys*.

Prep time: 5 minutes

Cooking time: 3 minutes @ each patty (Even if you are roasting more patties, each will still take 3 minutes to brown).

Total time: 8 minutes

Paneer Tikki (Cottage Cheese Patties)

Ingredients

Paneer (Cottage Cheese)-500 grams (18oz)

Bread pieces-2

Chopped Onion-1

Green chillies (chopped and de-seeded)-2

Cumin seeds (*Jeera*)-1/2 teaspoon

Chopped Fresh Coriander Leaves-A small bunch

Sugar-1/2 teaspoon

Garam Masala-1/2 teaspoon

Salt to taste

Cooking Oil-2 tablespoon

Method

Mash the *Paneer* well.

Soak the bread pieces in water. Squeeze the water from the bread with both hands and then add to the mashed *paneer*.

Add all the other ingredients and mix well.

Shape the mashed *paneer* mixture into small flat patties.

In a shallow non-stick pan, heat the cooking oil and place the patties.

Brown the patties evenly on both sides and remove to a dish covered with an absorbent paper napkin.

Repeat till all the patties are cooked.

Serve hot with chutneys.

Prep time: 5 minutes

Cooking time: 3 minutes @ each patty (Even if you are roasting more patties, each will still take 3 minutes to brown).

Total time: 8 minutes

Chutneys (Indian Home Made Sauces)

These are really mouth-watering sauces that can be made fresh, in smaller quantities without using any preservatives or other chemicals that the commercially made sauces come loaded with. These really go well with *Pakoras* and *Tikkis*.

Do, however, refrigerate these *Chutneys* and try to use up within a week.

Tomato chutney

Ingredients

Large ripe Tomatoes-5

Dates de-seeded-50 grams (2oz)

Sugar-1 cup

Salt-1/2 teaspoon

Cumin seeds (*Jeera*)-1/2 teaspoon

Saunph (fennel seeds)-1/2 teaspoon

Mustard Oil (or your preferred oil)-1 teaspoon

Red dry chili whole de-seeded (just for flavour and not to make it hot)-1

Method

In a wok, heat the oil and add the fennel, cumin seeds and the red chilli.

As soon as the mixture crackles (which takes only a few seconds), add the tomatoes. Please make sure that the mixture doesn't burn otherwise your *chutney* will taste awful!!!

Stir the tomatoes well and add the sugar and salt.

When the tomatoes are almost done, add the dates and cook for a few minutes more.

If the *chutney* becomes too thick, you may add a little water but this is not necessary.

Your tomato *chutney* with dates is ready.

Have it with *pakoras, tikkis* or even with your full Indian meal platter, as I like it.

Prep time: 5 minutes

Cooking time: 10 minutes

Total time: 15 minutes

Dhania Pudina Chutney (Coriander Mint Chutney)--Sweet Version

This is the JIFFIEST sauce on earth as it is prepared without cooking anything.

All the natural vitamins and anti-oxidants too, therefore, are fully preserved which makes this quite a nutritious *chutney*.

Ingredients

Green Mint Leaves-100 grams (3.5oz)

Green Coriander Leaves-100 grams (3.5oz)

Whole De-seeded Green Chilli-1

Tamarind (made into paste)-50 grams (2oz)

Sugar-4 tablespoon

Salt-1/2 teaspoon

Crushed cumin seeds (*Jeera*)-1/2 teaspoon

Method

Grind together all the ingredients in a grinder.

Take the mixture out in a bowl and taste to see if the sugar and salt is to your liking.

That's all!

Your *Dhania Pudina chutney* is ready, to be eaten with any snack or main dish.

Prep time: 5 minutes

Cooking time: Nil

Total time: 5 minutes

Dhania Pudina Chutney (Coriander Mint Chutney)--Salty Version

Ingredients

Green Mint Leaves-100 grams (3.50z)

Green Coriander Leaves-100 grams (3.50z)

Whole De-seeded Green Chilli-1

Lemon juice-2 tablespoon

Salt-1/2 teaspoon

Method

Grind together all the ingredients in a grinder.

Take the mixture out in a bowl and taste to see if the salt is to your liking.

That's all.

Your *Dhania Pudina chutney* is ready, to be eaten with any snack or main dish.

Prep time: 5 minutes

Cooking time: Nil

Total time: 5 minutes

Raita

Raitas are yoghurt based dishes that are served with the main meal in Northern India. You take a spoonful of this once in a while basically to cleanse your palate.

Again, you don't have to cook anything!

Apple Raita

Ingredients

Yoghurt-400 grams (14oz)

Grated Apple-1

Chaat Masala-1/2 teaspoon

Black Salt-1/4 teaspoon

Cumin seeds (pre-roasted and crushed)-1 teaspoon

Salt-1 teaspoon

Sugar-4 teaspoon

Method

In a bowl, whisk the yoghurt well with all ingredients EXCEPT THE GRATED APPLE.

Now add the grated apple and mix well.

That's all.

Your Apple Raita is ready.

Prep time: 5 minutes

Cooking time: Nil

Total time: 5 minutes

Cucumber Raita

Ingredients

Yoghurt-400 grams (14oz)

Cucumber-1 cut into bite size pieces

Cumin seeds (pre-roasted and crushed)-1 teaspoon

Salt-1 teaspoon

Sugar-2 teaspoon

Method

In a bowl, whisk the yoghurt well with salt, sugar and the roasted cumin seeds.

Add then the cucumber pieces.

That's all.

Your Cucumber Raita is ready.

Prep time: 5 minutes

Cooking time: Nil

Total time: 5 minutes

Pineapple Raita

Ingredients

Yoghurt-400 grams (14oz)

Canned pineapple-4 slices cut into bite size pieces

Cumin seeds (pre-roasted and crushed)-1 teaspoon

Salt-1 teaspoon

Sugar-4 teaspoon

Method

In a bowl, whisk the yoghurt well with salt, sugar and the roasted cumin seeds.

Add then the pineapple pieces.

That's all.

Your Pineapple Raita is ready.

Prep time: 5 minutes

Cooking time: Nil

Total time: 5 minutes

Raita with Mint and Coriander Leaves

Ingredients

Yoghurt-400 grams (14oz)

Chopped Mint leaves-20 grams (1oz)

Chopped Coriander leaves-20 grams (1oz)

Chaat Masala-1/2 teaspoon

Black Salt-1/4 teaspoon

Cumin (pre-roasted and crushed)-1 teaspoon

Salt-1 teaspoon

Sugar-4 teaspoon

Method

In a bowl, whisk the yoghurt well with all ingredients EXCEPT THE CHOPPED MINT AND CORIANDER LEAVES.

Now add the leaves.

That's all.

Your *Raita* with Mint and Coriander Leaves is ready.

Prep time: 5 minutes

Cooking time: Nil

Total time: 5 minutes

CHAPTER 10

OUR SWEETHEARTS

Indians are said to be born with a sweet tooth. Greek writers in the days of Alexander the Great had marvelled at how ordinary looking "reeds" in India could yield a substance that would be sweeter than honey.

So it is established that sugar from sugarcane was gifted to the world by India. Even the knowhow of sugarcane cultivation and processing was spread (mostly forcibly!) to all parts of the world, from Mauritius to the Caribbean, by Indian workers.

It is natural, therefore, to expect that all regions of India would have a very strong dessert making tradition. Sweets have to be offered to Gods and exchanged among friends on all auspicious occasions. Any good news, even in corporate offices, would result in a clamour for some exchange of sweets much to the bewilderment and bemusement of the foreigners around that place.

Most of such sweetmeats, as anywhere else in the world, would be prepared by *Halwais* (professional sweet makers) in commercial outlets. So a "Home Style" tradition of making desserts should legitimately raise some eyebrows.

Why, as elsewhere, this craft of making desserts at home has still not died out in India? I asked around and learnt that the first reason is the older generation's mistrust of anything commercial. So if you want to ensure that whatever ingredients you are using are unadulterated, especially when you are making sweets for an auspicious occasion, you will make these with your own hands.

The second, more practical reason is that this is the only way to regulate the sugar content or to enable the use of sugar substitutes in your desserts.

And finally, you still make desserts in Indian homes because you can make them in a JIFFY, without pre-heating ovens and waiting for hours for your stuff to bake.

It is in this background that I present 12 mouth-watering recipes that include 3 *Halwas*, 4 *Kheers*, 2 puddings and 3 sweets.

And believe it or not, all of these are regularly made in my home even today.

Besan Halwa (Chickpea Flour Dessert)

This dessert is fit for the Gods, literally, and so is offered quite frequently in temples.

Ingredients

Chickpea flour (*Besan*)-1 cup

Sugar-1/2 cup

Clarified butter (Ghee)-1/4 cup

Milk-1 cup

Saffron-few strands dissolved in milk

Green Cardomom-2 crushed

Cashew nuts-25 grams (1oz)

Raisins-25 grams (1oz)

Method

In a wok, add the clarified butter and put it on your heat source.

As soon as the clarified butter warms up, add the *besan* (Chickpea flour) and cashew nuts and stir till all become light brown and give off a lovely aroma.

Do please ensure that you don't burn the flour!

Add the sugar, milk along with the saffron, the cardamom and raisins to the flour.

Stir well till the dessert (*halwa*) dries up.

That's all.

Your Besan Halwa is ready.

Prep time: 5 minutes

Cooking time: 7 minutes

Total time: 12 minutes

Suji Halwa (Semolina Dessert)

This one is not offered to the Gods but tastes divine nonetheless.

Ingredients

Semolina (*Suji*)-1 cup

Sugar-1/2 cup

Clarified butter (Ghee)-1/4 cup

Milk-1 cup

Saffron-few strands dissolved in milk

Green Cardomom-2 crushed

Method

In a wok, add the clarified butter and put it on your heat source.

As soon as the clarified butter warms up, add the semolina (*suji*) and stir till it becomes light brown and gives off a lovely aroma.

Do please ensure that you don't burn the semolina!

Add the sugar and the milk along with the saffron and the cardamom to the semolina.

Stir well till the dessert (*halwa*) dries up.

That's all.

Your *Suji ka Halwa* is ready.

Prep time: 5 minutes

Cooking time: 7 minutes

Total time: 12 minutes

Aatey Ka Halwa (Whole Wheat Flour Dessert)

Ingredients

Whole Wheat Flour dessert (*Atta*)-1 cup

Sugar-1/2 cup

Clarified butter (*Ghee*)-1/4 cup

Milk-1 cup

Saffron-few strands dissolved in milk

Green Cardomom-2 crushed

Raisins-1 tablespoon

Cashew nuts-2 tablespoon

Method

In a wok, add the clarified butter and light the flame.

As soon as the clarified butter warms up, add the wheat flour (*atta*) and the cashew nut.

Stir till both become light brown and give off a lovely aroma.

Do please ensure that you don't burn the flour!

Add the sugar, raisins and the milk along with the saffron and the cardamom to the wheat flour.

Stir well till the dessert (*halwa*) dries up.

That's all. Your whole wheat flour dessert (*atta ka halwa*) is ready.

Prep time: 5 minutes

Cooking time: 7 minutes

Total time: 12 minutes

Chawal Ka Kheer (Rice Pudding)

This is again a North Indian dessert that the Gods are very fond of. So don't be surprised to be served this *Kheer* with *Pooris* outside Hindu temples, even outside India.

Ingredients

Full cream milk-1 litre (2 US pints liquid)

Rice-2 heaped tablespoon

Sugar to taste - (start with 3 tablespoons)

Milk Powder-2 tablespoons

Green Cardomom-2 crushed

Saffron-few strands (optional)

Method

In a heavy bottomed wok, bring the milk to boil.

Add the rice which should have been washed well.

Keep stirring on low heat making sure that NOTHING BURNS.

As the mixture begins to thicken, add the milk powder, sugar, the cardamom and the saffron.

Stir well and keep stirring for about 5 minutes.

Switch off the heat source.

That's all. Your delicious *Kheer* (Rice Pudding) is ready.

You can either have it hot as some like it. Or you could let it cool down and then put it in the fridge and have it when it is cold.

Prep time: 1 minute

Cooking time: 20 minutes

Total time: 21 minutes

Natun Gud Ka Kheer (Rice Pudding with Palm Jaggery)

This is an out-of-this-world dessert from Eastern India with such subtle flavours that you will just fall in love with.

Ingredients

Full cream milk-1 litre (2 US pints liquid)

Rice-2 heaped tablespoon

Palm Jaggery (crushed) - 3 tablespoons

Milk Powder-2 tablespoons

Method

In a heavy bottomed wok, bring the milk to boil.

Add the rice which should have been washed well.

Keep stirring on low heat making sure that NOTHING BURNS.

As the mixture begins to thicken, add the milk powder.

Stir well and keep stirring for about 5 minutes.

Switch off the heat source and add the palm jaggery.

Stir well.

Note: DON'T add the palm jaggery when the milk is still on the fire as this may curdle the milk.

That's all. Your *Natun Gud Kheer* is ready.

You can either have it hot as some like it. Or let it cool down and then put it in the fridge and have it when it is cold.

Prep time: 1 minute

Cooking time: 20 minutes

Total time: 21 minutes

Sevai Kheer (Sweet Vermicelli Milk Pudding)

This is a very popular dessert of the Muslims in India who have to have it during *Eid*. A drier version called *Sevaiyyan* too, like its West Asian counterpart, is quite tasty.

Ingredients

Full cream milk-1 litre (2 US pints liquid)

Vermicelli (roasted)-1 heaped tablespoon

Ghee (clarified butter)-1 teaspoon

Sugar to taste - (start with 3 tablespoons)

Milk Powder-2 tablespoons

Green Cardomom-2 crushed

Raisins-25 grams or 1oz (optional)

Method

In a heavy bottomed wok, bring the milk to boil.

Keep stirring the milk on low heat making sure that it DOES NOT BURN.

As it begins to thicken, add the milk powder, sugar, and the cardamom.

Stir well and keep stirring for about 5 minutes and remove from fire.

In a pan, heat the Clarified butter (*Ghee*) and add the vermicelli.

Gently toss the vermicelli for about a minute.

Note: *Ghee* is just for flavour. So you can avoid it if you are cutting down on calories.

Add the vermicelli to the wok containing the thickened milk. You may add raisins if you so desire.

Boil for a minute. Switch off the heat.

Let the dish set for about 10 minutes.

That's all.

You can either have it hot as some like it. Or let it cool down and then put it in the fridge and have it when it is cold.

Prep time: 2 minutes

Cooking time: 20 minutes

Total time: 22 minutes

Ghola Prasad or Aatey Ka Kheer (Whole Wheat Flour Porridge)

This is not really porridge but the closest dish that it comes close to, in the West, is porridge. This dish is usually eaten in Eastern India especially during some religious festivals where it is better known as *Ghola Prasad* (literally dissolved blessings).

It is also a complete meal in itself and is really filling if you have it for breakfast. Also, the browned whole wheat flour in milk imparts a really nice aroma which is very appetizing. A perfect alternative of a traditional porridge, I must say.

You may try this variation of a porridge if you are getting bored with eating cereals or traditional porridges for breakfast.

Otherwise treat this as an Indian dessert and enjoy.

Ingredients

Whole wheat flour-1 cup

Sugar-1/2 cup

Clarified butter (*Ghee*)-1 tablespoon

Milk-3 cups

Green Cardomom-2 crushed

Cashew nuts-50 grams (2oz)

Raisins-25 grams (1oz)

Almonds-25 grams (1oz)

Walnuts-25 grams (1oz)

Dried figs-25 grams (1oz)

Dried Dates-25 grams (1oz)

Method

In a wok, add the clarified butter and put it on your heat source.

As soon as the clarified butter warms up, add the wheat flour and stir till all become light brown and give off a lovely aroma.

Do please ensure that you don't burn the flour!

Switch off the flame.

Remove the wok and pour the browned flour in a bowl.

Mix together the browned flour, sugar, milk along with the cardamom and the other dry fruits.

Mix well and let the mixture cool for at least half an hour before serving.

That's all. Your *Ghola Prasad or Aatey Ki Kheer* is ready.

Prep time: 5 minutes

Cooking time: 5 minutes

Total time: 10 minutes

Fruit Pudding

Ingredients

Full cream milk-1 litre (2 US pints liquid)

Sugar to taste - (start with 3 tablespoon)

Milk Powder-2 tablespoon

Chopped Fresh seasonal fruits-1 cup

Raisins--25 grams (1oz)

Mixed Nuts-50 grams (2oz)

Method

In a heavy bottomed wok, bring the milk to boil.

Keep stirring on low heat making sure that it DOES NOT BURN.

As the milk begins to thicken, add the milk powder and the sugar.

Stir well and keep stirring for about 5 minutes.

Switch off the heat source.

When the mixture cools a little, add the fresh fruits, raisins and nuts.

Let it cool down further and then put the pudding in the fridge.

Have it when it is cold.

Your delicious fruit pudding is ready.

Prep time: 5 minutes

Cooking time: 20 minutes

Total time: 25 minutes

Custard Pudding Indian Style WITHOUT EGGS

When you have less time or don't have the patience to thicken milk, this is another alternative you can try for turning out a delicious fruit pudding.

Ingredients

Full cream milk-1 litre (2 US pints liquid)

Sugar to taste - (start with 3 tablespoon)

Corn Flour-3 tablespoon

Vanilla/Orange essence-3 drops

Chopped fresh seasonal fruits-1 cup

Raisins--25 grams (1oz)

Mixed Nuts-50 grams (2oz)

Method

Dissolve the corn flour in ½ cup milk.

In a heavy bottomed wok, bring the rest of the milk to boil.

Add the dissolved corn flour to the milk.

The milk will immediately start getting a thick consistency.

Switch off the heat source.

When the mixture cools a little, add the fresh fruits, raisins, nuts and the essence.

Let it cool down and then put the pudding in the fridge.

Have it when it is cold.

Prep time: 5 minutes

Cooking time: 5 minutes

Total time: 10 minutes

Sandesh (Cottage Cheese Sweet)

This is the classic Eastern Indian sweetmeat that Bengalis are so fond of.

Ingredients

Fresh *Paneer* (cottage cheese)-1/2 kg (18oz)

Sugar-250 grams (9oz)

Milk Powder--3 tablespoons

Green Cardamom-3 crushed (OR few drops of Vanilla or any food flavour that you like.)

Method

In a thick bottomed wok, mix together all the ingredients.

Note: If you are using any essence/food flavour other than cardamoms, then don't add that now as heat may dilute or destroy that. Do, however, remember to add this flavour before you put it all in the food processor.

Place the wok on your heat source.

Keep stirring till all the water dries up and the consistency becomes thick.

Pour it all into a food processor and blend well.

Pour the mixture into a big plate or serving dish and let it cool down.

Now pick up small portions and make it into any shape with your hands (or using any moulds).

That's all. Your *Sandesh* is ready.

Prep time: 5 minutes

Cooking time: 10 minutes

Total time: 15 minutes

Natun Gud Sandesh (Cottage Cheese Sweet with Palm Jaggery)

This is yet another legendary Eastern Indian sweetmeat that Bengalis just love.

Ingredients

Fresh *Paneer* (cottage cheese)-1/2 kg (18oz)

Palm jaggery-150 grams (5oz)

Sugar-100 grams (3.5oz)

Milk Powder--3 tablespoons

Method

In a thick bottomed wok, mix together all the ingredients.

Place it on your heat source. Keep stirring till all the water dries up and the consistency becomes thick.

Pour into a food processor and blend well.

Pour the mixture into a big plate or serving dish and let it cool down.

Now pick up small portions and make it into any shape with your hands (or using any moulds).

That's all.

Your *Natun Gud Sandesh* is ready.

Prep time: 5 minutes

Cooking time: 10 minutes

Total time: 15 minutes

Kachha Gola (Sweet Cottage Cheese Balls)

This too is a classic Eastern Indian or rather Bengali sweetmeat

Ingredients

Fresh *Paneer* (cottage cheese)-1/2 kg (18oz)

Sugar-250 grams (9oz)

Milk Powder--3 tablespoon

Rose water-few drops

Method

In a thick bottomed wok, mix together all the ingredients EXCEPT ROSE WATER.

Place it on your heat source.

Keep stirring till all the water dries up and the consistency becomes thick.

Pour the mixture into a big plate or serving dish and let it cool down.

Add the rose water.

Now pick up small portions and make it into any shape with your hands (or using any moulds).

Traditionally, it is made like small balls.

Your *Kacha Gola* is ready.

Prep time: 5 minutes

Cooking time: 10 minutes

Total time: 15 minutes

CHAPTER 11

DRINKS

What Indians are very fond of drinking is, you guessed it, just plain water. Not flavoured, not effervescent, just pure aqua is what the residents of this tropical region have to have with every meal.

Sure, there have been all kinds of local brews, from fermented rice or barley (*Chhang*) that is popular in Ladakh and Sikkim, to the Toddy that is consumed in the coastal areas, to the ones made from *Mahua* flowers which is what the tribals have, and how can you forget the potent *Feni* which is made from the waste of Cashew fruit, that the Goans have.....the list could be endless.

The huge marketing efforts of multinationals have also borne fruit and Indian now guzzle zillion cases of whiskeys, rum, vodka, gin and wine, you name it.

But all this is drunk before you eat your food, which is the opposite of what you do in the West.

Many have tried teaching Indians how to pair wines with Indian curries and well, to be polite, they are still trying.

So I'll leave the multinationals to their strategies and focus on some "Home Style" drinks, if I may dare call them that, that Indians have no problem having with their meals or before it, any time of the day or night.

I present in that background 11 JIFFY drinks: 6 Shakes, 2 Coffees, 2 Lassies, and one Lemonade.

Mango Milkshake

Ingredients

Ripe Mango--2 (In case fresh mangoes are not available, you can use canned mango pulp. In that case it will be 2 cups of pulp)

Milk-500 ml (2 cups approximately)

Vanilla ice cream--3 scoops (optional)

Sugar to taste

Method

If you are using fresh mangoes, remove the skin and the seed.

Chop the mango into small pieces and blend it in a blender.

(If you are using canned mango pulp, you can naturally skip this step).

Place both the milk and the mangoes in the freezer for about half an hour so that they become really cold.

After that, blend together the cold milk, the mangoes and the sugar, preferably in a blender/mixer.

In large glasses, put a scoop of vanilla ice cream (optional) first and then pour the milk shake over it. This helps blend the two flavours, vanilla and mango, better.

(Otherwise just pour the blended milk and the mangoes in a large glass and enjoy.)

Prep time: 7 minutes

Cooking time: No cooking time

Total time: 7 minutes

Instant Mango Shake

If you don't have enough time to make a conventional mango shake as described above, or you can't get hold of either fresh or canned mangoes, you can try this shortcut method and still enjoy your mango shake.

Ingredients

Mango juice-1 can or 1 small tetra pack (cooled to freezing point)

Vanilla ice cream-2 scoops

Method

In a blender, blend together the mango juice and the vanilla ice cream.

Blend well.

Pour into a glass and your instant mango shake is ready.

Prep time: 5 minutes

Cooking time: No cooking time

Total time: 5 minutes

Banana Shake

Ingredients

Ripe Banana--1

Milk-250 ml or 1 cup (chilled to freezing point)

Sugar to taste

Method

Peel the banana and blend it in a blender till the banana gets a paste like consistency.

Add the sugar and the cold milk.

Blend again till the milk and the banana are well blended.

Pour into a large glass.

Prep time: 5 minutes

Cooking time: No cooking time

Total time: 5 minutes

Kiwi shake

Ingredients

Ripe Kiwi-2

Milk-250 ml or a cup (chilled to freezing point)

Sugar to taste

Method

Peel the kiwis and blend it in a blender till it gets a paste like consistency.

Add the sugar and the cold milk.

Blend again till the milk and the kiwis are well blended.

Pour into a large glass.

Prep time: 5 minutes

Cooking time: No cooking time

Total time: 5 minutes

Strawberry shake

Ingredients

Fresh strawberries chopped-1 cup

Sugar-1/2 cup

Chilled Milk-200 ml (1 cup)

Vanilla ice cream-2 scoops

Method

Please note that fresh raw strawberries simply crushed in milk DO NOT TASTE GOOD. Therefore, it is suggested to make a strawberry preserve to make your milkshake taste heavenly.

How to create the strawberry preserve:

In a pan, cook together the fresh strawberries and the sugar till the strawberry is slightly cooked.

Cool the preserve and refrigerate it for future use.

The quantity made is a little more than what is required for a single milk shake but making even lesser quantity of strawberry preserve may be a bit tedious.

In a blender, blend together the chilled milk, 4 tablespoon approximately of cooled strawberry preserve, and one scoop vanilla ice cream, for about 3 minutes.

In a tall glass, add a scoop of vanilla ice cream first and then pour over it the strawberry shake.

That's all. Your heavenly Strawberry Shake is ready.

Prep time: 5 minutes

Cooking time: 5 minutes

Total time: 10 minutes

Mixed Fruit Shake

Ingredients

Fresh seasonal fruits (de-seeded, peeled and chopped)-1 cup

Milk-2 cups

Sugar to taste

Method

Cut and cool the fruits for at least ½ an hour before making the shake.

Similarly, the milk should be really cold near freezing point.

In a blender, blend the mixed fruits well till they get a paste like consistency.

Add the chilled milk and sugar and again blend well.

Pour into glasses and enjoy your Mixed Fruit Shake.

Prep time: 10 minutes

Cooking time: No cooking time

Total time: 10 minutes

Cold Coffee

Ingredients

Milk (any kind you like-skimmed, semi-skimmed, whole milk)--200 ml (1 cup)

Instant coffee-2 heap teaspoon

Sugar or any sugar substitute to taste

Ice crushed-100 ml (half a cup approximately)

Method

Chill the milk in the freezer till it reaches freezing point.

In a blender, add the coffee and the sugar and then add the milk.

Blend for a minute.

Add the crushed ice and again blend for about 3-4 minutes.

Pour into a tall glass and enjoy your frothy cold coffee.

Prep time: 2 minutes

Cooking time: No cooking time

Total time: 2 minutes

Cold Coffee with ice cream

Ingredients

Milk (any kind you like-skimmed, semi-skimmed, whole milk)--200 ml (1 cup)

Instant coffee-2 heap teaspoon

Sugar or any sugar substitute to taste

Vanilla Ice cream-2 scoops

Method

Chill the milk in the freezer till it reaches freezing point.

In a blender, add the coffee and the sugar and then add the milk.

Blend for a minute.

Add one scoop of ice cream and again blend for about 3-4 minutes.

In a tall glass, add a scoop of ice cream and pour the blended coffee over it.

Enjoy your cold coffee with vanilla ice cream.

Suggestion: You may even choose to add a cap full of coffee liqueur to this for added flavour and kick.

Prep time: 3 minutes

Cooking time: No cooking time

Total time: 3 minutes

Mango Lassi (Yoghurt Mango Shake)

Ingredients

Ripe Mango--2 (In case fresh mangoes are not available, you can use canned mango pulp. In that case it will be 2 cups of pulp)

Yoghurt-500 ml (2 cups approximately)

Crushed ice--200 ml or a cup (Crush the ice before hands in a food processor/or by any other method so that it blends well with the yoghurt).

Sugar, or sugar substitute, to taste

Method

Remove the skin of the mango and also the seed.

Chop the mango into small pieces.

In a blender, blend the pieces.

Now place both the yoghurt and the mangoes in the freezer for about half an hour so that they become really cold.

Blend together the cold yoghurt, the mangoes, sugar and the crushed ice. Mix well.

In large glasses, pour the blended yoghurt (*Lassi*).

Your delicious Mango *Lassi* is ready.

Prep time: 7 minutes

Cooking time: No cooking time

Total time: 7 minutes

Rose Flavoured Lassi

This is the most popular *Lassi* that you can ask for in any North Indian restaurant.

Ingredients

Yoghurt-500 ml (2 cups approximately)

Crushed ice--200 ml or a cup (Crush the ice before-hands in a food processor/or by any other method so that it blends well with the yoghurt).

Sugar, or sugar substitute, to taste

Rose essence- (few drops) or Rose water-1 tablespoon

Method

In a blender, blend together the yoghurt, crushed ice, sugar and rose essence/rose water.

Mix well.

Pour into large glasses.

That's all. Your Rose Flavoured *Lassi* is ready.

Prep time: 2 minutes

Cooking time: No cooking time

Total time: 2 minutes

Nimboo Pani (Lemonade Indian Style)

Ingredients

Juice of Fresh Lemon-1

Sugar-2 tablespoon

Pinch of salt

Water-250 ml or a cup

Method

In a glass, mix the sugar with ½ the quantity of water.

When the sugar is dissolved, add rest of the water, the lemon juice and a pinch of salt.

Mix well.

That's all. Your Indian Lemonade (*Nimboo Paani*) is ready.

You can substitute water with plain Soda for the restaurant version of this drink.

Prep time: 2 minutes

Cooking time: No cooking time

Total time: 2 minutes

CHAPTER 12

SEQUENCING, PARALLEL PROCESSING AND PLANNING A FULL INDIAN MEAL

L et us admit it frankly. Laying out a full Indian meal looks daunting, even to Indians.

Take an example from my own home. A typical EVERYDAY (emphasis mine!) meal here would usually consist of a rice or Indian bread, a *dal* (lentil), a curry (vegetarian or non-vegetarian) and a dry vegetable dish. I leave out the accompaniments and desserts as they would always be there in the fridge and could be added at a moment's notice if anyone felt the need to do that.

How much time do you think we would be spending on putting together this basic four-dish Indian platter that I just described above? At least two hours?

What will you say if I claim that we manage to do that in 30 minutes on an average? Impossible? So let me prove how it is NOT impossible.

But before we do that, let me take up those two big words SEQUENCING and PARALLEL PROCESSING that I started with from this chapter's heading. It is absolutely vital that we employ the full force of these two tools to help us achieve our objective.

Sequencing is to know what comes first and then next, in a natural, logical manner. So when you wear your socks and then your shoes, you just sequenced your actions in a very natural manner without even thinking about it.

You can further improve the quality of your sequencing by planning and anticipating. So if you are going out to party and have made up your mind about what dress you would be wearing, you should also select your shoes and socks and keep them readily accessible than leave this decision to the last minute. Going backwards, you should also check if your dress is ironed and your shoes polished.

Applying this common sense to cooking would mean that once you have decided what you would like to cook, you should gather all ingredients and wash, dry, chop, or blend them in the order they would be required in the recipe. French call this *mise en place* or putting it in place. You certainly can't practice any cooking in a JIFFY without internalizing this first principle of intelligent cooking.

Parallel processing is the art of juggling two or most tasks at the same time without hopefully affecting the quality of any. So listening to music while driving is parallel processing that we all practice with ease. In cooking, this would mean that while you put one dish to cook, you start chopping, blending or whatever for the next dish and so on.

I am sorry if I'm still sounding confusing and worse, bombastic. So without further ado, let me give a real example of how using the two techniques of sequencing and parallel processing, we can put together a complete Indian meal of four dishes on the table in less than 30 minutes.

Suggested Full 4-dish Foundation Meal*: Rice, Arhar Dal (split pigeon pea lentils), Keema Mattar (lamb/chicken mince curry with peas) and Aloo Gobi (potato-cauliflower) dry vegetable.*

First, the obvious, collect all ingredients as per the recipes already given.

Next, ready all the needed vessels and appliances.

Now, measure and wash the rice and let it dry.

Wash the dal and put it in the pressure cooker along with water, turmeric, and salt. Fire up your heat source and place the cooker on it.

Cut the tomatoes, and add to the dal.

Now close the lid of the pressure cooker and let it cook on high heat.

While *dal* is cooking (in the pressure cooker that doesn't require your frequent supervision), cut the onions, ginger, garlic and tomatoes for both the *Keema Mattar* and the *Aloo Gobi*.

For *Keema Mattar*, make a paste of its share of onion, ginger, garlic, tomato in the blender.

Now cook the *Keema Mattar* (in the second pressure cooker).

The dal may have cooked by now. So switch off your heat source and let the pressure cooker cool down.

Put the potatoes and cauliflower for steaming in the microwave.

Put the rice to cook (in the third pressure cooker, otherwise use the other options described in the recipe).

While rice is cooking (in a pressure cooker that doesn't require your frequent supervision), start cooking the *Aloo Gobi* dish in a wok in parallel.

Your *dal* pressure cooker may have cooled down by now. If not, force cool the cooker under running cold water and open the lid. Now put *tadka* (temper) to the dal.

As each dish is cooked, transfer it to an insulated casserole. This helps keep the food warm and you can eat piping hot food (all four dishes together, and without any reheating) in the next two-three hours.

This is how it is all done in my home every day in less than half an hour.

Naturally this requires practice and familiarity with the cuisine you are handling. You certainly can't do it if you are trying out these dishes for the first time in your life.

But then who said cooking is a race to be completed within 30 minutes? And what will happen if you cook dishes in lots, say, two the previous evening and two now? After all, don't you stock desserts and sauces in your fridge beforehand? For that matter, who says you have to have four dishes at the minimum to constitute a proper Indian meal? Will heavens fall if you just have a 1-dish *Khichdi*, a complete meal in itself that is considered fit for offering to the Gods; or the popular 2-dish *Poori* and a curry dish?

Did you also notice that my JIFFY meal above used three pressure cookers, one each for rice, dal and *Keema Mattar*, one wok for the *Aloo Gobi*, a blender and a microwave with steamer attachment? Now we in our home have invested in these vessels and appliances because we need them every day.

But if you are a just an occasional fan of Indian cuisine, then naturally it will not be feasible to invest in so many pressure cookers, for example. So use whatever you have. I have already given some alternative ways of cooking without pressure cookers but I'm sure you can discover more ways to do so with your favourite vessels and appliances.

The simple point is that if you plan well, sequence your actions and cook some dishes in parallel, you could rustle up your meals quite in a JIFFY.

MEAL PLANNING AND PARTING TIPS...

Keeping the 4-dish structure intact, you could have infinite variations of my "Home Style" Indian platter. For example, you can substitute the plain rice dish with any of the six other types of rice dishes, or with any of the three breads that are there in Chapter 5.

You could similarly substitute the *Arhar Dal* with any of the nine other *dals* that I cover in Chapter 6; the *Keema Mattar* with any of the eleven other fish & fowl dishes of Chapter 8; and the *Aloo Gobi* with any of the fourteen other vegetable dishes mentioned in Chapter 7.

You could try some less complicated combinations too. For example, if you choose to have any of the *Pulaos,* you may realize that you don't need a *dal* with it. Instead, you can do quite well with just a curry and a dry dish, making this option a 3-dish platter.

Similarly, if you choose one of the special Indian breads like *Poori* or *Paratha*, you may like to have this with just one dry or curry dish, and not requiring the dal again. That will make this a 2-dish platter and still quite a delicious one at that, ask any Indian.

And if you choose to stick with a dish like *Khichdi*, which is a complete meal in itself, you may like to add just *Aloo Bharta* and *Tomato Chutney*. Of course, if you are serving *Khichdi* on a festive occasion, then you may add *Baigun Bhaja*, pickles and some roasted *papadums* as well. That will make this a lavish 6-dish platter and you can still claim that you are "fasting" to appease God *Shani* (Lord Saturn)!

I am not a mathematician but the short point I am trying to make is that there could literally be thousands of such permutations and combinations of the basic Indian platter. And then there would be those endless possibilities of slipping in an Indian dish or two in a proper Western 3-course dinner, which is already happening. You may have already seen a rice pilaf paired with roast chicken or a Chicken Tikka Masala with garlic toast.

So let your imagination run riot and let a thousand flowers bloom.

Bon appétit.

Note: Let me assure you that any kind of cuisine anywhere in the world would be eminently suitable for such planning, sequencing and parallel processing. In my college dorm, as I have described in my Book "How To Cook In a Jiffy Even If You Have Never Boiled An egg Before", I bumbled into making a proper 3-course meal in less than 30 minutes. Want to know how (without buying my first book)? Here is the full excerpt:

EXCERPTS FROM "HOW TO COOK IN A JIFFY: EVEN IF YOU HAVE NEVER BOILED AN EGG BEFORE" (CreateSpace; First Edition; 8 October 2013, pages 164—to 171)

Making a Full Lunch or Dinner in less than 30 minutes

You may use the art of proper sequencing and parallel processing to make Chicken soup, breaded baked chicken, sautéed vegetables and garlic toast in less than 30 minutes. Don't believe it. Let me prove it to you then.

Basic Chicken Soup

Ingredients

Chicken stock—2 cups

Boiled shredded chicken-50 grams (2oz)

Grated Cheese-25 grams (1oz)

Milk-1/2 cup

Corn Flour-1 heap tablespoon full

Salt and Pepper to taste

Sugar-1/2 teaspoon

Method

Make the chicken stock by boiling chicken using the following method:

Take 500 ml water and pour the water in a pan and add salt to taste.

Submerge the chicken in the water inside the pan.

Place the pan on fire and let the water come to boil.

Reduce the heat and let the chicken simmer for about 10 minutes.

It is advised that you check that the chicken has been cooked properly. This can be done by using a fork to prick the chicken to see whether it has been thoroughly cooked.

Take the pan off from the heat source.

Now, take the chicken out and keep it on a separate plate once the water has cooled.

Shred some portion of the chicken into bite size pieces (50 grams or 2oz) and keep the rest for your breaded baked chicken.

Keep the chicken stock in the same pan.

Add the cheese, sugar and salt.

Switch on your heat source and put the pan on it.

Bring this mixture to a boil.

Meanwhile, dissolve the corn flour in half a cup of milk separately.

Add this to the mixture in the pan to give it a nice creamy taste.

Boil for 2 more minutes and add the shredded chicken.

A trick is to taste the soup to see whether the salt is alright or whether you need to add a little more.

Your chicken soup is ready.

Breaded Baked Chicken

Ingredients

Boiled chicken piece-2 (any piece breast, leg, or thigh with or without bones)

Two slices of bread toasted and crushed into crumbs

Egg-1

Wheat Flour-1 tablespoon dissolved in half a small cup of water for coating the chicken

Salt-Just a pinch

Utensils-Baking tray, oven, a bowl and a pan to boil the chicken

Method

First, make the bread crumbs if you don't have it in ready stock. For making bread crumbs, you can take some left over bread which is already a little hard. Toast it well in the toaster. Take it out and let it cool down a bit. Then take a spatula to beat the toast till it all turns into crumbs.

Break the egg by gently tapping the middle portion of the egg with a fork till a crack appears. Keep tapping till the crack becomes a small hole. Gently press the egg to break it into two halves. Pour the liquid in a bowl.

Mix the egg and wheat flour together and add a little salt.

In another plate, keep the crushed bread. Take the chicken piece one by one and coat them first in the egg and wheat flour mixture and then coat with the bread crumbs.

Put these on a baking tray and bake in a pre-heated oven at 150 degrees Celsius for 15 minutes. Your non-deep fried, healthy Breaded Chicken is ready.

If you don't have access to an oven, you can simply deep fry the breaded chicken a´ la KFC.

Sauté Vegetables

Please feel free to use any seasonal European vegetable---- this list is only indicative.

Ingredients

Cauliflower-100 grams (3.5oz)

Broccoli-100 grams (3.5oz)

Carrot-100 grams (3.5oz)

French beans-100 grams (3.5oz)

Peas shelled or snow peas-100 grams (3.5oz)

Butter-1 tablespoon

Water-2 tablespoon

Salt and Pepper to taste

Method

Wash the vegetables thoroughly.

Wherever needed, cut in bite size pieces.

Switch on your heat source and put a pan on it.

Add the butter to the pan and let it melt.

Add all the vegetables and stir well.

When the vegetables start changing colour, add a pinch of salt and keep stirring.

Reduce the heat to minimum (SIM on a gas stove), add the water and cover the pan.

You will see that the steam starts escaping after a while.

Keep checking till the water has dried.

Tip: You may also use a fork to poke the vegetables to ensure that they have been cooked properly.

Your sauté vegetables are ready. At this stage, you may like to add some pepper.

Garlic Toast

Ingredients

Bread-2 slices preferably cut thick (you can use any bread, or even bun of your choice)

Garlic-5 cloves crushed

Salted Butter-20 grams (1oz)

Any fresh green herb of choice

Method

In a pan, warm up the butter and add the crushed garlic.

Let it cook for a minute and then switch off.

Meanwhile, toast the bread (or bun) well.

Spread the garlic mixture on the toast.

You can sprinkle any fresh herbs on this toast.

Your delicious garlic bread is ready.

Let's now come to the sequencing and parallel processing needed for your lunch or dinner

First of all, gather all your ingredients and vessels.

Then begin with the soup.

While the soup is cooking, sauté the vegetables in a separate pan and toast the bread for the breaded baked chicken.

Once this is done, toast the bread/bun lightly for the garlic toast.

While the chicken soup is cooling down, transfer the vegetables to a casserole.

Finish the soup and put it in a casserole if you want the soup to remain piping hot.

Make the breaded chicken and put it in the oven.

Make the butter + garlic spread. Put the spread on the toast for the garlic toast.

Take out the chicken from the oven.

Your lunch/dinner is ready in a JIFFY, in less than 30 minutes.

You can make lots of dishes with your boiled chicken, many of which do not require an oven, and substitute that dish for the breaded chicken. This will add more variety to your lunch/dinner menu without much effort. **(END OF EXCERPT)**

OTHER BOOKS BY THE AUTHOR

HOW TO COOK IN A JIFFY EVEN IF YOU HAVE NEVER BOILED AN EGG BEFORE

Introducing "How To Cook In A Jiffy"— The Easiest Cookbook On Earth From The Author Of The Hugely Popular Website www.cookinginajiffy.com

Never boiled an egg before but want to learn the magic art of cooking? Then don't leave home without this Survival Cookbook. Be it healthy college cooking, or cooking for a single person or even outdoor cooking---this easiest cookbook on earth teaches you to survive all situations with ease.

Where this book scores over other "How To" cookbooks is the structured manner in which it follows a step by step "graduation" process.

Most uniquely, the book teaches the concept of "sequencing and parallel processing" in cooking to enable busy people to create a 3-4 course meal in less than 30 minutes.

The book is fun and entertaining to read with the author sharing his own personal story of bumbling about in the wonderlands of cooking, with wit and humour.

Recommends Amazon.com reviewer B. Farrell "*This is a good informative book for someone starting out in the adventure of cooking. This would make a great gift for a young bride just starting out with her new duties of cooking or a single person getting out on their own.*"

CONNECT WITH THE AUTHOR

This book has been written, I believe, in such a way that even an absolute newbie should not have any problems following it. However, if you do encounter some problem or find any portion confusing, then feel free to write to me anytime at ciaj@cookinginajiffy.com.

If you liked this book and want to hear from us again regarding news of upcoming books or if you wish to receive weekly recipes and cooking tips from us, then you may want to subscribe to our blog. You can do that by simply going to our website cookinginajiffy.com and registering.

I would love to connect with you on Social Media.

Join me on Facebook at https://www.facebook.com/cookinginajiffy or follow me on Twitter at https://twitter.com/CookinginaJiffy

You can even find me on Goodreads at http://www.goodreads.com/prasenjeet

ABOUT THE AUTHOR

 Prasenjeet Kumar is a Law graduate from the University College London (2005-2008), London University and a Philosophy Honours graduate from St. Stephen's College (2002-2005), Delhi University. In addition, he holds a Legal Practice Course (LPC) Diploma from College of Law, Bloomsbury, London.

Prasenjeet loves gourmet food, music, films, golf and traveling. He has already covered sixteen countries including Canada, China, Denmark, Dubai, Germany, Hong Kong, Indonesia, Macau, Malaysia, Sharjah, Sweden, Switzerland, Thailand, UK, Uzbekistan, and the USA.

Prasenjeet is the self-taught designer, writer, editor and proud owner of the website cookinginajiffy.com which he has dedicated to his mother.

PLEASE REVIEW MY BOOK

If you have liked my book, then I shall be grateful if you could leave a review on the site from where you purchased this book and show your support.

INDEX

Made in the USA
San Bernardino, CA
27 December 2013